BEATTOCK

The Anatomy of a Dumfriesshire Parish

by

Frank Ryan

Dumfries and Galloway
Libraries, Information and Archives
2007

First published 2007

© Publication copyright Dumfries and Galloway Libraries, Information and Archives.
© Text copyright Frank Ryan.

All rights reserved. No part of this work may be reproduced, stored in a retrieval system, or transmitted, in any form or by any means, electronic, mechanical, photocopying, recording or otherwise, without the written permission of Dumfries and Galloway Libraries, Information and Archives.

Printed in Scotland by Solway Offset *the* Printers, Dumfries for the publisher:
Dumfries and Galloway Libraries, Information and Archives
Central Support Unit, Catherine Street
Dumfries DG1 1JB
Tel: 01387 252070   Fax: 01387 260294
www.dumgal.gov.uk/lia

Libraries, Information and Archives is a section of Cultural Services which is an operational unit within the Community Services Group of the Department of Education, Social Work and Community Services.

ISBN 978-1-946280-75-4

A complete list of our publications is available from the above address or on our website at www.dumgal.gov.uk/lia. Our e-mail address is libs&i@dumgal.gov.uk

Preface

A book about Beattock!
It sounded like a tall order when Robert Smith, a third generation Beattock man of farming stock, invited me to tackle the task of writing it. I wondered how I would find enough material to fill a chapter let alone a whole volume. After all, at first glance, Beattock is little more than one street. It hardly gets a mention in guidebooks or gazetteers and is rarely in the news.

I can count on the fingers of one hand the number of times I rushed off to the area on a story when I was the southwest Scotland correspondent for a national newspaper.

Usually the call was to a road accident but I remember a local shepherd being marooned in a snowstorm, a train crash, a leak in the natural gas pipeline and, much earlier, an interview with famous long-distance walker Dr Barbara Moore when she stopped at Beattock House Hotel, as it then was, on her trek from John o' Groats to Land's End. Little else springs to mind.

To me, Beattock was just a sleepy hamlet on the road to Glasgow... but that was before I began to dig into its past and to explore the surrounding parish of Kirkpatrick Juxta.

Every community has a story to tell and the Beattock area is no exception. Romans, roads and railways all play a part in its history. Border reivers and warring landowners have added blood and plunder to the script. And, as I discovered, there are many quirky and fascinating characters and odd episodes along the way.

Would it surprise you to know that the author of arguably the most important document in the history of Scotland was a Kirkpatrick Juxta man and that Beattock boasts among its famous sons a pioneer of the British television industry, an author of rip-roaring tales, a famous brewer and an international footballer? Did you know the area has links with royalty, not to mention a female Braveheart? And what's the story behind Hoppertitty and Toot Corner?

This book is not a history or a guide, more a series of snapshots. It aims to capture the flavour of the place, bring to life something of its past and capture its present. It owes a great deal to the local people who gave of their time to provide information and reminiscences and to the ever-helpful staff in the reference department at the Ewart Library in Dumfries.

Thanks to them all.

Frank Ryan
November 2007

BEATTOCK AS IT WAS: (top) Porteous' garage at the north end of the village in the early days of the car; (centre) local residents pose for a picture in front of J & D Locke, bootmakers; (bottom) the local post office, once a key feature of village life.

Contents

Preface		3
Chapter 1	Village At The Crossroads	7
Chapter 2	The First Settlers	20
Chapter 3	They Came, They Saw	22
Chapter 4	Clan Carnage	26
Chapter 5	Highway Dramas	33
Chapter 6	Beattock For Moffat	44
Chapter 7	Kirks, Ministers And Ghosts	59
Chapter 8	All The Stats	67
Chapter 9	The Big Hoose	74
Chapter 10	Focus On Farming	77
Chapter 11	Famous Folk	85
Chapter 12	I Remember, I Remember	105
For Further Reading		111

BEATTOCK'S main street has a deserted look in this picture from the early years of last century.

Village at the Crossroads

Whizzing by road or rail across the Solway Plain just north of the Scotland-England Border, modern travellers do not even catch a glimpse of Beattock. The sleepy little village is tucked away off the motorway and its once busy rail station has long since disappeared. Those who spot the name Beattock on a sign, may associate it with the station where trains once had to stop before getting a shunt up the notoriously steep Beattock Summit but it is a safe bet that most who pass by have never heard of it.

TUCKED away in Evan Valley, Beattock is hardly noticed by travellers who speed by on the A74(M) or the London-Glasgow rail line.

Yet this rural settlement on Evan Water - the only village in oddly-named Kirkpatrick Juxta parish in the north of Dumfriesshire - is at the centre of an area that has been an arena for much of Scotland's turbulent history.

The story of Beattock has to be told in the context of the wider countryside where in succeeding eras Celtic tribes, Roman legionaries, Robert the Bruce, Covenanters, Jacobites, English armies and other invaders have all left their mark.

Long before the village of Beattock existed, the beautiful valley of the Evan Water, which rises in Lanarkshire and flows into the River Annan, was a strategic route from the south to the

Beattock

Scottish Lowlands - the gateway to the north. It has remained so throughout the centuries. The remnants of a large number of hill forts, enclosures and peel towers testify to its strategic importance.

The early inhabitants took advantage of the hilly terrain to build their defensive farms and, when the Romans came, legionaries established camps and fortresses to secure their captured territory and built a road through the valley for marching from Solway to Clyde

The Romans' influence on the area lasted for more than 200 years but towards the end of the period the local tribes were left very much to their own devices. When the legions left in the 4th century, the inhabitants of South Scotland who survived were part of a Romano-Celtic world. Some of the tribes had formed alliances with the occupying forces and there were Roman names in the pedigrees of their chiefs. Some of the people were professedly Christian.

There were hill settlements probably occupied by chiefs and large round farmhouses surrounded by palisades. In the West the kingdom was once ruled by Coel Hen (the original Old King Cole). His descendants controlled the province of Rheged, thought to have extended from Galloway to south of Carlisle. But the tribes were disunited and were soon crushed by the Angles from the great kingdom of Northumbria who opened a way to the Solway and pushed north along the river valleys.

After two centuries, however, their influence also began to wane for a variety of reasons - Celtic resistance, internal dissensions, Scandinavian invasions. The decline of the Angles made way for the Celtic people - Picts, Scots and Britons - to begin the long process of uniting as one nation. Around 843 AD Kenneth MacAlpin, King of Scots, gained the throne of Pictland and by 1018 Malcolm II had taken over Lothian. Sixteen years later Duncan I was King of a united Scotland.

After the Norman Conquest the power of the Crown extended to south Scotland. In the 1120s, King David granted Robert de Brus the Lordship of Annandale and 200,000 acres. Two centuries later, his famous ancestor Robert the Bruce would gain Scotland's freedom and the throne. King David also placed Norman retainers in mottes or moated manors to rule over the area and the first churches were established. It is around this time that Kirkpatrick Juxta begins to be identified. Eventually, a parish was defined, bordered by Closeburn, Moffat, Wamphray, Johnstone, Kirkmichael and Lanarkshire in the northwest.

The medieval period was marked by strife, battery and bloodshed as the West March of the Anglo-Scottish Border became what has been described as "a veritable cockpit" of local feuds between powerful families like the Johnstones and the Maxwells, as well as national wars - proof that the land was worth fighting for and defending. The constant plundering and pillage, however, turned the so-called Debatable Land into a wasteland. English travellers well into the 18th century described the stretch of country from the Border to Moffat as "a dreadful desert".

While the area is steeped in history and dotted with ancient sites, Beattock itself is comparatively modern. It did not begin to emerge until the 18th century though variations of the name existed for hundreds of years before that. It came into prominence in the early 1800s when a new road designed by famous engineer Thomas Telford was constructed through the area. The Brig Inn, an important staging post for mail coaches, was opened at the junction of the new route and the existing Dumfries-Moffat road, and Beattock became a key point on the road network.

The village-at-the-crossroads gradually developed along the highway, which, as the A74, remained the main road link between England and Scotland till the 1960s. It became a thriving country centre serving the needs of the surrounding agricultural area. The 1841 census for Kirkpatrick Juxta shows that the parish with 42 farms and a population of 932 (including five octogenarians) must have been virtually self-sufficient. It boasted five blacksmiths, six shoemakers, six masons, two millers, five tailors, five joiners, five handloom weavers, four dressmakers, two gardeners, two road surfacemen, a cooper, stocking maker, forester and piano tuner. There were seven apprentices in the various trades.

It was the coming of the trains a few years later, however, that gave Beattock its greatest boost and earned its enduring reputation as a railway village. As the depot for the fleet of pug engines that pushed freight and passenger trains over the challenging Summit in the age of steam, it was the base for a large railway workforce. The parish population in 1851 rose to the highest in its history - 1096.

AN early picture of Beattock's main street shows how little its appearance has changed.

Beattock

Beattock is an amalgam of three hamlets: Craigielands, on the west side of the main street, comprised a dozen cottages built to accommodate staff on Craigielands estate, originally owned by the famous Younger brewing family. Houses on the opposite side, known as Beattock Park, originally belonged to the other local mansion Beattock House and were built in the second half of the 19th century. Finally there is the Back Village to the west of the main settlement. The Caledonian Railway Company constructed about 20 workers' houses that apparently had a distinctive smell because of the old kerosene-coated sleepers used as fuel. More properties were added around 1859 under a scheme by the Hope Johnstones, of Raehills, descendants of the powerful Johnstone family who had dominated the area for centuries. The idea was to provide homes at the joint expense of proprietor and tenant. They were leased at five shillings (25p) a year. At this time, the Hope Johnstones owned more than 100 properties in the parish.

Over the next century, the population of the parish declined and as farming became more mechanised workers moved from agriculture to other jobs especially on the roads and the railways.

Two world wars brought changes to Beattock and the surrounding area. The parish lost 24 men in the Great War and was involved in rehousing Belgian refugees and in a scheme to provide sphagnum moss for dressing wounds at the front.

DAD'S ARMY, Kirkpatrick Juxta-style . . . 24 men and one women were the last bulwark against Hitler.

Village at the Crossroads

During World War 2 training camps were established around the parish including a target range on Beattock Hill. Older residents remember how the whole village shook when the artillery was fired. Dykes at Kinnelhead and Wester Earshaig suffered as tanks rumbled over the countryside.

Six men and one woman from the parish were killed in World War 2. They are all commemorated along with those from the 1914-18 conflict on a war memorial in the churchyard.

In 1947 a youth club was formed in Beattock with activities ranging from choral singing to leatherwork and drama. The community council was launched a year later and is still in existence.

Sheila G. Forman, writing in the Third Statistical Account in 1958 reported that several farms and cottages had electric light - it had first been introduced in 1933 - and telephones, and most families had a wireless "while a number of

AS these pictures show, Kirkpatrick Juxta School had a much bigger roll last century than the present primary.

Beattock

MATCHETT'S GARAGE stood on a strategic site at the junction of the old A74 and the Dumfries Road

television masts have appeared since 1956".

She added: "New houses are still needed and a number of railwaymen employed at the station and the line have to live in Moffat. No building societies are patronized... most cottages are let at reasonable rents but tenants would like to have improved sanitary conditions." In the worst cases, she reported, sanitation was "very primitive" with some houses in the village having dry toilets.

Beattock School with 70 pupils was "well provided with teaching apparatus, including a sound cinematograph projector and a radiogram relayed to both classrooms" - a far cry from today's IT equipment. Thrift was encouraged by a National Savings group and the school had a branch of the county library "which is very much used".

The second half of the 20th century saw Beattock transformed from a bustling road and rail junction into a quiet backwater. The Beattock-Moffat rail link closed in 1954, the village was by-passed in the 1960s and the rail station closed a decade later. First the co-operative store, then the village shop and post office were shut down and the local policeman was not replaced when he retired.

In 1965, a large proportion of Annandale Estates was sold to pay for inheritance tax after the death of Evelyn Wentworth Hope Johnstone at the age of 85 the previous year. A total of 13 farms, grass parks and woodlands, comprising over 23,000 acres went under the hammer.

Today, the once thriving parish has a population of just over 500, no shop, post office or filling station, no village bobby. The two garages - run by the Matchett and Porteous families - have disappeared.

Village at the Crossroads

BEATTOCK today . . . a sleepy community off the beaten track and (below) as it was a century ago.

Beattock

> One of the quaintest place-names around Beattock is **Toot Corner**. It is a bad bend on the narrow road from the gate of Dumcrieff House to near Moffat and is so called, according to locals, because drivers have to toot their horn before turning the corner. It is mentioned in the official guide to the Southern Upland Way which described the road beside the Evan Water as an "interesting diversion" off the main route.

On the up side, the village is on a bus route linking it with Dumfries and Moffat. It still has its hall, nearby parish kirk and primary school (although not in the original building and with a roll of just about 40), the Brig Inn until recently still flourished as a hotel with an appropriately named Telford Restaurant but now there are plans to convert it into two maisonettes and two flats. However, the village has a new pub, the Old Stables Inn.

Tourism is beginning to play a major role in the parish. The grounds of Craigielands mansion have become a caravan and camping park with bar,

SIGN OF THE TIMES: the grounds of Craigielands House are now a holiday park.

Village at the Crossroads

THE village hall has been a centre for local activities since it was gifted by the Forman family of Craigielands.

Beattock

BEATTOCK HOUSE, a mansion on the east side of the village, was once a hotel and now has holiday chalets in the grounds.

restaurant and well stocked loch for anglers. At the time of writing, log cabins for holidaymakers are being built in the grounds of Beattock House.

There is a retreat centre in the former Lochhouse Farm, offering self-catering and bed and breakfast accommodation, and several other guest houses in the area.

Up the Crooked Road at the north end of Beattock, there are plans for an outdoor adventure centre on the former sheep farm of Kinnelhead - once the biggest in the parish, covering 8,500 acres of rugged terrain and moorland, it aims to offer a wide range of activities suitable for all ages, including quad bike safaris to explore the wildlife, clay target shooting, falconry displays and hawk walks.

The village has also expanded with five new housing estates, all developed after World War 2.

Although there is no local manufacturing industry in Beattock, there are some links with commerce and industry. The village is the site of a British Gas compressor station for two interconnectors supplying natural gas from Scotland to Ireland. Another pipeline, owned by Shell Chemicals UK, also passes through the area, carrying ethylene from Grangemouth to Stanlow in Cheshire.

Beattock has another claim to fame - it is on the Southern Upland Way, the long-distance footpath, stretching 212 miles from Portpatrick on the southwest coast to Cockburnspath on the eastern seaboard. In the official guide, Ken Andrew describes "the glorious view" across Annandale that unfolds on the approach to Beattock from the west. He writes: "The Evan Water winds across the plain but the Annan is difficult to see. There is plenty of other variety in the bounded fields, multiplicity of tree-belts, scattered farms, rural houses and the square tower of Lochhouse dominated by the high hills cleft by the valley of the Moffat Water.

"Most walkers will relish Annandale as a diversion from the lonely moors, forest and ridges they have encountered and will quicken their step to join in the action as they stride down the Crooked Road. Even those who dislike civilisation will feel keyed up with anticipation as they view the distant tracks winding up into the Ettricks where the Way progresses."

Away from the long-distance footpath, there is a wealth of beautiful countryside in Kirkpatrick Juxta - rolling hills, wide sweeping valleys, picturesque glens and the winding Kinnell, Garpol and Evan Rivers. The Upper Annandale parish is part of the Southern Uplands that have been described as the Highlands in miniature. The countryside is less dramatic but none-the-less appealing.

Despite this, Beattock, it has to be said, has never enjoyed a particularly good press in guidebooks or elsewhere.

What's in a **name**? Several derivations have been given for the name **Beattock**. James B. Johnston in his Place-Names of Scotland claims it comes from the Gaelic biod-ach and means sharp or top place while Jamieson's Scottish Dictionary says the name signifies a piece of land between two burns.. Sir Edward Johnson-Ferguson in his Place Names of Dumfriesshire only tells us that the second syllable appears to be Old English hoc - a hook or bend - but gives no details of the first syllable. So, it's a case of take your choice.

Johnson-Ferguson lists the various versions of the name Beattock that have appeared over the centuries - from Baithuke in 1489 to Betok, Baithdok, Badok, Bathok and Batok at different times in the 16th century and Baitok in 1625.

Beattocks, by the way, is an old Scots word for mashed potatoes but its origin is not known.

Beattock

Sir Denis Forman, who was born and brought up in Craigielands, gives a somewhat biased description of the village in the early 20th century in his autobiography *Son of Adam.*

"Beattock village is no more than a strip of semi-detached but-and-ben cottages on each side of the main Glasgow Road," he wrote. "The west side of the village belonged to us, the east side to Beattock House. Our side had the village shop, the village hall, the smithy and its emergent garage. Their side had nothing. Our side shone white with lime wash, the steps 'redd up' with soft red chalky stone; their side was plain granite and scruffy."

The Craigielands side, he boasted, had a wide variety of personalities and surnames; the other side was clannish. He tells how once when a stranger inquired for a Mr Moffat on the Beattock Park side, he got the reply: "Moffat? There's naebody of that name on this side. We're all Johnstones and Jardines here." Which, according to Forman, was approximately true.

Is there a link between **Beattock Rise** in north London, and its Dumfriesshire namesake? Beattock Rise is a quiet residential street in Muswell Hill in the borough of Haringey.

A search of the Haringey archives produced no information about how the street got its name. But there is a railway connection, which could be significant.

The street runs alongside Northern Heights Parkland Walk which follows the course of a disused branch line, linking Highgate with Alexandra Palace Station. Not unlike the Beattock-Moffat spur, it was opened 10 years earlier and closed by British Railways in the same year, 1954. While the Dumfriesshire single track was for the benefit of visitors to Moffat's Hydropathic Hotel, the London line was a direct route to Alexandra Palace.

The Palace burned down two weeks after it opened and the line was closed for two years while it was rebuilt. Is there a rail link between Beattock and Beattock Rise - or is it just coincidence? Maybe someone out there knows the answer.

There is also, by the way, a Beattock Street in the Partick district of Glasgow.

Village at the Crossroads

Gazetteers are not much kinder to the village. They either ignore it altogether or dismiss it with a throwaway sentence. The Borders Counties volume in The Queen's Scotland series, edited by Theo Lang, for instance, comments only that Beattock is little more "than a kind of back door to Moffat, the place where the traveller turns off the Glasgow-Carlisle road and the railway junction for Moffat."

Beattock, it is true, has always been in the shadow of its more elegant neighbour Moffat, once famous and fashionable as a spa town and still a favourite venue for visitors. Yet, in a more gritty way, Beattock had its day thanks to the railways. Now tourism is offering a chance of prosperity in the future.

The First Settlers

Although it is not possible to say exactly when Man first arrived in the area now known as Kirkpatrick Juxta, there is archaeological evidence that primitive hunter-gatherers roamed the countryside as early as 5000BC. Originating in the countries around the Mediterranean, these Stone Age people travelled from the West and over Queensberry, the 2285-foot high rounded hill that forms the Western barrier of the present-day parish. They were nomads who favoured thinly wooded terrain because of their lack of heavy timber-cutting tools and survived by tracking down wild deer, boar and oxen. Stone axes have been found in the parish and there is a stone burial chamber - a scheduled ancient monument - from this era at Stiddrig Farm, Beattock.

At some time before 2000 BC the first farmers emerged with their polished flat axes and mattock-blades. They settled in the fertile river valleys and, judging by the rich heritage of fortress and burial cairns, the area appears to have been relatively well populated in the Bronze and Iron Ages. The Royal Commission on Ancient and Historical Monuments and Constructions of Scotland in its 1920 report recorded no fewer than 18 forts, three motes, three enclosures and 10 cairns in Kirkpatrick Juxta parish and others have been discovered since then.

The forts, generally round or oval in contrast to the later square or oblong Roman fortifications, were built mostly on hills which afforded them a clear view of the surrounding land and were often protected by ramparts and ditches giving them a show of strength - all-important to the warlike Celtic tribes. Some of the forts occurred in clusters - for example on Beattock Hill and at Gardenholm near the Edinburgh-Moffat road. Their close proximity made it possible for them to warn one another about the approach of an enemy by lighting beacons.

Three Standin' Stanes on the road between Beattock and Moffat . have been interpreted in various ways by archaeologists over the years.

It has been suggested that they indicate the site of a battle or mark the spot where three officers fell. Both suppositions, it is now believed, are improbable and experts now believe the stones could be of druidic origin.

The First Settlers

The forts were surrounded by open landscapes of pastures where earlier dense forests had been cleared and where cattle, sheep and pigs were reared and crops like wheat and barley were cultivated. Like most of the Iron Age people in Britain, these early communities that grew up around the Evan and the Kinnell were self-sufficient farmers and craftsmen who produced their own clothes, pots, tools and weapons. The settlements were ruled over by warriors, the protectors and champions of the tribe, key elements in the structure of Celtic society.

The largest and most important hill fort in Kirkpatrick Juxta was on the summit of Beattock Hill, 851 feet above sea level, overlooking the vale of Upper Annandale. The oval-shaped fort occupied the whole of the summit and measured about 213 feet by 100 feet. It was encircled by a massive stone wall, now entirely ruined. It has been suggested that Beattock Hill fort, which looks directly towards Burnswark across 16.5 miles of countryside, could have been a signalling point used by early tribes.

The forts were outnumbered by the cairns dotted around the area. Varying in diameter from about 12 to 42 feet they are generally accepted to have been last resting places or memorials for the illustrious dead from the settlements. Many of them are around Kinnellhead far up in the moorland that stretches from Beattock Hill to Queensberry. Only one long cairn has been found - nearly 900 feet up in the moors about five miles south of Beattock. It measures 91 feet by 61 feet.

The forts obviously posed a threat to the Romans and, it has been argued, their existence could have been one reason for the building of Hadrian's Wall.

Many of Kirkpatrick Juxta's **archaeological finds** are exhibited at Dumfries Museum.

They include the so-called Stidriggs horde - a lead container with tool implements, believed to be late Iron Age or early medieval. They were found on Stidriggs farm in 1985.

Other finds include several coins, a brooch and a dolphin figurine all from the Roman era, a Bronze Age witch stone used to ward off witches, a flint arrowhead and an old horseshoe from Craigielands Smithy.

They Came, They Saw…

The heavily armed and highly disciplined Roman legionaries who trudged through Scotland more than 1900 years ago left their footprint on Kirkpatrick Juxta

As in other parts of the country, they constructed roads for the movement of troops, reinforcements and supplies, set up marching camps as staging posts and built forts and fortlets where garrisons could defend the occupied territory against aggressive local tribes. The occupation was purely military; Kirkpatrick Juxta could boast no grand Roman villas or bath-houses like those in other conquered territories.

The military buildings and encampments in the Beattock area have long since gone, razed by centuries of cultivation. Today, they are recognisable only from crop marks surveyed from the air. Some artefacts have been discovered - an axe, hobnails from boots, iron harness pieces, a gate lock, a small jar. But they tell us little about the day-to-day life of the Roman army or the nature of the forts with their bath houses, statues of deities and, outside the gates, civilian communities of local women and slaves with whom the soldiers - forbidden to wed while on military service - associated and had children.

Contemporary written accounts are also sparse, apart from the work of the historian Tacitus who described the campaign of his father-in-law Gnaeus Julius Agricola in the 1st century AD.

The most significant evidence of the Roman incursions into the Beattock area is to be found at Milton farm, about a mile south of the village. The site, on the crest of a low ridge running down the middle of the Annan valley, has been explored over the years by archaeologists who have given us some idea of what the fortifications looked like and how they were used in the 1st and 2nd centuries AD. Archaeologists, however, are extremely cautious academics who pepper their reports with words like "possibly" and "probably" and inevitably the picture that emerges is sketchy and speculative. The most likely interpretation of the explorations is that there was a heavy Roman reconnaissance of the area around 70AD with the main incursions beginning about a decade or so later.

The Milton fortifications were first recorded by General William Roy, the military engineer who was given the task of drawing an accurate map of Scotland after the Battle of Culloden in 1746. He gave the fort the name of Tassieholm from an adjoining hamlet, which no longer exists, but today it is commonly called Milton after the farm.

The most extensive exploration of the site was begun by archaeologist John Clarke in 1938 and after being interrupted by the war was resumed in the summer of 1946 and continued till 1951.

Clarke and his team of university students found traces of two forts, one on top of the other, dating back, they believed, to the reign of Emperor Titus

Flavius Vespasianus in the 1st century AD when the fighting general Gnaeus Julius Agricola, governor of Britain from 78 to about 84AD, pushed the northern frontier of the Roman empire into what is now Scotland. According to his son-in-law, the historian Tacitus, they were operating within the territory of 'new tribes' who do not appear to have offered serious resistance to the Roman advance.

In a series of campaigns, culminating in the rout of the Caledonian tribes at the Battle of Mons Graupius - believed to have been fought near Inverurie, Aberdeenshire, in AD 84 - Agricola consolidated his conquests by building fortresses at strategic points.

Milton, a gateway to the shortest route into the lowlands, appears to have been the site of one of these vital defences. A fortified enclosure in a neighbouring field, Clarke concluded, may have been linked to the fort that was obviously a substantial building with one or two granaries, two double barrack blocks and workshops.

Like other fortresses from this so-called Flavian period, it is likely to have been evacuated or destroyed after Agricola was recalled to Rome around 84AD by Emperor Domitian who down-sized the British legions to three and virtually abandoned the Scottish conquests, leaving local tribes like the Brigantes and Selgovae to take control of the land.

Clarke's team also unearthed traces of a Roman presence dating from the post-Flavian period. On the Milton site, he discovered signs of a fortlet that could have been an outpost for Hadrian's Wall - built from the Tyne to the Solway between 122AD and 127AD as an 80-mile long defensive axis. It is known that forts were established on both sides of the wall.

In a nearby field there was also evidence of a road-post, typical of the many that served as stations for small garrisons, each responsible for policing about 40 miles of highway. This building almost certainly belongs to the era of Emperor Antoninus Pius whose governor of Britain Quintus Lollius Urbicus subdued the territory north of Hadrian's Wall once again and built a 37.5 mile defensive system in the early 140s from the Forth to the Clyde - the so-called Antonine Wall.

Clarke's work was all on the ground. He did not have the benefit of surveys from the air that were introduced after World War 2. They added a vast wealth of detail, confirming that the Milton fort was only one element in a sequence of defences. Aerial photography of crop markings also identified at least five camps originally described as "temporary" or "marching camps" where, it was thought, legionaries would erect their serried rows of leather tents - each made from over 30 calf skins - for rest periods of no more than three nights as they advanced. The most recent researchers, however, have questioned this theory.

Three of these camps were located about three-quarters of a mile north of the Milton fort. The most extensive, about 29 hectares in area, lies on the south bank of Evan Water. Its gateway defences and the fact that it is not aligned with the Roman road running through the area convinced archaeologists that it was established in the Flavian era.

The other two camps, occupying 14.6 and 11.5 hectares both on the opposite bank of the Evan, are thought to be from the same period. A fortlet known as Barnhill partly overlies the north-east angle of the smaller camp. Researchers believe it dates from the Antonine period and was possibly garrisoned by a detachment of the 1,000-strong cavalry unit, the 2nd Cohort of Tungrians from Belgium, based at Birrens, near Lockerbie, one of the largest and most important Roman forts in the area - known to its occupants as Blatobulgium ("the flour sack").

The most recent excavations in the Beattock area were carried out at the camp south of the Evan by Glasgow University Archaeological Research Division in July and August 1994 in advance of the upgrading of the A74 Glasgow-Carlisle trunk road.

In a report published in 1995, team leaders Keith Speller and Alan Leslie conclude that the site represented rather more than a short-stay marching camp. They speculate that it could have been a construction camp for the fort at Milton or, perhaps more likely, an early campaign base for troops operating in this part of south-west Scotland.

They based this on evidence that the camp had been allowed to stand undisturbed for an indefinite length of time. The discovery of "an unmistakable Roman field oven" also seemed to imply a certain duration of occupation. The archaeology team was unable to put a date on the camp and acknowledged that further investigations are necessary.

With the advance into Scotland in the 140s, the Roman army is believed to have taken a tighter grip on South Scotland than previously. Yet despite fieldwork and aerial reconnaissance since the end of World War 2 no other forts have come to light in Kirkpatrick Juxta from this period. The same is true of the following 250 years. Although the Romans withdrew from Scotland after the death of Antoninus Pius in 161, they returned on several occasions to put down uprisings but again there is no confirmed evidence of any camps on the western route into Scotland. Following the death of the Emperor Septimus Severus at York in 211 AD his son Caracalla made peace with the tribes of the north and withdrew from Scotland and there is no mention of unrest on the northern frontier until the end of the next century when campaigns began against the Picts and the Scots who were harassing the northern frontier. After the so-called Barbarian Conspiracy of 367 all the outpost forts were abandoned and the Roman army finally conceded even nominal control of Kirkpatrick Juxta and the surrounding area.

Beattock's near neighbour, the hamlet of **Hoppertitty**, has one of the oddest names in Dumfriesshire and over the years controversy has raged about its origin. Local tradition claims it is derived from the Latin 'oppidum Tatius' meaning the town of Tatius, a Roman general under Agricola. But experts do not accept this derivation. Professor Bill Nicolaisen, author of Scottish Place Names, stated in an article in The Scots Magazine in 1964, that it is "absolutely impossible" for the first part of the name to have come from the Latin oppidum and he also discounts any connection with a Roman general. Such a survival would be unique among Scottish place names, he said and pointed out that the original version of the name in 1873 was Hoppertoody and it was not until 1900 that it was linked to Tatius in Forrest's Illustrated Guide to Moffat. Nicolaisen concluded that the name derives from a nickname but offered no further explanation.

He also claimed that another local place name Tassie Holm had no connection with Tatius. He referred to earlier spellings - Thasselholm, Tassyisholme and Tashawholm - and argued that it was much more likely to be connected to the surname Tait as this family was linked with the land in the area, probably as early as 1573. Rev James Johnston is his Place Names of Scotland gives the derivation of Tassie Holm as "probably from the Gaelic tais meaning moist, damp or soft" and holm, a riverside field.

Researcher W.A.J. Prevost supported Nicolaisen's view. In a newspaper article in 1976 he observed that there is no reference to Hoppertitty before 1873. Furthermore, he revealed, there is a Happertittie Burn near Birkhill, about 10 miles north-east of Moffat - an area where no Roman general ever built a town.

Hoppertitty Dry Dock, by the way, is a local name-joke, like Palnackie Treacle Works in the Stewartry and Gasstown Harbour in Dumfries. The phrase was apparently coined by a local retired gentleman who lived in the area.

Clan Carnage

Two ancient buildings near Beattock are reminders of the Mafia-style vendettas that raged between Border clans in medieval times. Lochwood Castle, of which little remains, and Lochhouse Tower, restored and still occupied, were strongholds of the Johnstones, the family who dominated Annandale for centuries. Their long-running blood feud with the powerful Maxwells of Nithsdale is described by author George MacDonald Fraser in *Steel Bonnets*, the story of the Border reivers or freebooters as the "bitterest and bloodiest" family quarrel in British history - including even those of the Highlands. At one stage the two clan chiefs each offered a grant of land to anyone who would bring him the head or hand of the other.

The Johnstones were among the most ancient and most powerful of the Border septs. The 'rough-footed clan,' as they were called, with a winged spur as their emblem and 'Aye Ready' as their motto, originated in East Lothian. The first of the family on record was Sir John de Johnstone, one of the Scottish barons who swore allegiance to Edward I of England, in 1296. His great-grandson, of the same name, was conspicuous for his valour in the defence of Scotland in the reigns of David II and Robert II. In 1370 he defeated an English invading army and two years later was appointed one of the guardians of the Western Marches. His son, also Sir John, got 300 of the 40,000 francs sent by the King of France in 1385 to be divided among the Scottish nobles to induce them to carry on hostilities against their common enemy, the English. His son, Sir Adam Johnstone, was one of the commanders of the Scottish army at the Battle of Sark in 1448, in which they gained a signal victory over the English invaders. He also took a prominent part on the royal side in the desperate struggle between James II and the Douglases, and was instrumental in suppressing their rebellion against the Crown. He was rewarded with a grant of the lands of Pettinane, in Lanarkshire and the Johnstones have ever since borne along with their ancestral arms the heart and crown of Douglas as a memorial of the important service rendered to the royal cause. Sir Adam's eldest son was the progenitor of the Annandale or main branch of the family.

The Johnstones' power struggle with the Maxwells, which had been smouldering for generations, flared towards the end of the 16th century when the two clans were rivals for supremacy of the Scottish Western Border, a lawless frontier ravaged by reivers or riding families - rustlers, outlaws and gangsters who lived by terrorism, blackmail, extortion and murder.

The Warden of the Western March had the unenviable task of keeping order in the Borderland but the post was extremely lucrative. Part of the fines and forfeits imposed in warden's court went to him and forage and rations were allocated to him and his retinue. The post switched with bewildering regularity between successive chiefs of the Johnstones and the Maxwells, many of whom were outlawed, imprisoned, killed or deposed. The fierce rivalry was fuelled by mutual jealousy and hatred and by the intervention of forces from south of the Border who wanted to secure Dumfriesshire for the English Crown. The constant warring turned the Debatable Land - the territory claimed by both Scotland and England - into a wasteland.

Lochwood Castle

Lochwood Castle was the chief seat of the Johnstones in those days of 'rugging and riving'. Its position in the midst of bogs and morasses made it a fortalice of great strength, and led to a remark attributed to James VI that 'the man who built it must have been a thief at heart.' It first came into prominence as a stronghold of national importance in 1547 when Sir Thomas Carleton, of Carleton Hall, Cumberland, led a raid across the Border on behalf of the English Crown. Plundering and killing with a vengence, he and his band of "English, Scots and broken men" soon had Dumfries under their control but met strong opposition from the wild men of Galloway and had to use his silver-tongued persuasion to avoid a clash when he was cornered by Maxwell's private army. Taking refuge in Canonbie, he decided to seize Lochwood, temporarily under-garrisoned as a result of Lord Johnstone's recent capture by the English. According to Carelton's own account, a dozen of his men stole over the courtyard wall into the domestic quarters by night and "took the wenches and kept them secure in the house till daylight". The next morning, when one of the tower's depleted garrison ordered a girl to open the double door, Carleton's men broke too soon so that the girl leapt back into the tower and almost succeeded in closing the door again. The reivers prevented her, however, and in the skirmish that followed Carelton captured the tower which he found well stocked with salted beef, malt, butter and cheese.

Carleton was confirmed as Keeper of Lochwood and Governor of Annandale by Lord Wharton, Warden of the English Marches. With the tower as his power base, he "rode daily and nightly upon the king's enemies", looting, burning and taking prisoners. The surrounding area was laid waste and it was not until the treaty of Norham in 1551 that peace was restored. But it lasted less than 10 years as a tug o' war began over the Wardenship of the Western March. It had become almost a hereditary Maxwell post but John, the eighth Lord Maxwell was deposed in 1577 by the Regent, the Earl of Morton, for refusing to renounce his claim to the Morton title. He was replaced by the Laird of Johnstone, his principal rival who was given a royal commission to apprehend Maxwell on the grounds that he had maintained relations with the robber clan of Armstrong.

The Johnstones and the Maxwells were at each other's throats and the result was a brutal war that raged for months. Lands were wasted, crops destroyed, cattle driven off and houses burned by both sides. In 1585, Maxwell supported

Beattock

by 400 Armstrongs, Scotts, Beatties and Littles descended on Lochwood, sacked it and the surrounding houses, killed six Johnstones and took a dozen prisoners. He then torched the castle "that Lady Johnstone might have a light to set on her hood." In the raid, the Johnstones' charter kist was destroyed with all its contents including jewellery, writs and other documents - a great loss to the family and to history.

The Maxwells triumphed and Johnstone, the warden, was taken prisoner. But scarcely a month passed before Maxwell, an opponent of the Reformation, was in disgrace. He was accused of marching in procession to the College of Lincluden in Dumfries for the celebration of mass in public, and was arrested and imprisoned. He was released soon afterwards - on the occasion of King James' wedding to Anne of Denmark - and surprisingly on Johnstone's death the same year, was again appointed Warden.

Lochwood Tower was repaired and in 1592 it played host to James VI who spent a night there during a military expedition to quieten the Borders. Despite the royal peacemaking efforts, the feud between the Johnstones and Maxwells flared again the following year. They clashed at Dryfe Sands near Lockerbie in the Borders' last great clan battle, resulting in many Maxwells dead including the clan chief.

The King was back at Lochwood in 1602 during another peace-making mission into the Border country but still the great Johnstone-Maxwell blood feud raged. The last tragic act came in 1608 when a meeting arranged between Lord Maxwell and Sir James Johnstone to settle the families' differences ended in violence.

In a scene worthy of the Wild West, a bitter row broke out between the chiefs' companions, Charles Maxwell and William Johnstone. The former drew a pistol and shot the latter through the cloak. Lord Maxwell then rode after and shot Sir James. He managed to rise to his feet but Charles Maxwell delivered the coup de grace. The two murderers then rode off together.

"The horrible treachery of this crime, which it is difficult to believe was not premeditated, was too much even for the stomach of these times," writes Sir Herbert Maxwell in his *History of Dumfries and Galloway*.

Lord Maxwell escaped to France and after four years' exile ventured to return to Scotland though his lands had been forfeited and bestowed on others. He was betrayed by a relative, arrested, tried and executed in 1613, aged only 26. His younger brother became head of the clan and was within seven years restored to the possessions, titles and dignities of his predecessors.

Around this time Lochwood was modified and extended and in 1633 when Sir James Johnstone was raised to the peerage he took the title of Lord Johnstone of Lochwood. But the tower came to be subordinate to Newbie Castle near Annan as the family's principal residence. It was still in use at the end of the 1600s but by the beginning of the next century it was virtually abandoned and is said to have been destroyed by fire in 1710. The ruins of the once grand fortress remain the property of the Hope-Johnstones, the lineal descendants of the Marquesses of Annandale, who established their right to the dormant Earldom of Annandale and Hartfell in 1985. A full excavation of Lochwood Tower was carried out between 1982 and 1986.

Lochhouse Tower

Lochhouse Tower, which is still occupied, was in medieval times second only to Lochwood in importance as a Johnstone stronghold. Strategically situated where the waters of the Evan, Annan and Moffat converge, it stood on a slight eminence at the northern end of a loch from which it took its name and whose waters provided a natural defence to the south-east and south-west.

LOCHHOUSE TOWER, a 16th century stronghold, is still occupied today.

Beattock

It appears to have been built soon after the English occupation of Lochwood ended in 1550. It is not mentioned at that time but was firmly established when the important marriage contract between Margaret, daughter of John Johnstone of that Ilk and Edward, eldest son and heir of Edward Irving of Bonshaw, the Irving chief, was drawn up 'at the Lochhouse' in 1566. When Johnstone died the following year, the inventory referred to a hoard of gold and silver in a coffer at Lochhouse.

A year later in 1568, Johnstone's grandson and heir, Sir John Johnstone handed the tower to the Earl of Moray during his progress through the West March to enforce obedience to James VI after Queen Mary's defeat at Langside. He promised submission and the tower was saved.

In the 1630s, a dispute arose between James Johnstone and Viscount Drumlanrig over the superiority of the lands of Lochhouse. The issue was eventually resolved by the Privy Council in favour of Drumlanrig but the Johnstones continued to occupy the house for the next century. After that it ceased to be of importance and was eventually abandoned as the family seat. It was sold in 1879 to William Younger of Auchen Castle who also purchased the superiority. His son, Sir William Younger, the 1st Baronet, partially restored the roofless shell of Lochhouse around 1900 when the first two floors were modernised and covered with a flat roof. The tower was eventually sold as a separate house in 1978. The new owner replaced the roof and carried out further restoration work.

Auchencass

Auchencass is the only castle, as distinct from forts and peel towers, in the parish of Kirkpatrick. Its ruins, about a mile north west of Beattock, date back to the mid 13th century and in its day it was a fortress of great strength with walls 15 to 20 feet thick.

Standing on high ground between the Evan and the Garpol, commanding a wide view of Upper Annandale, it is believed to have been built by the Kirkpatricks as a successor to their Norman-style wooden motte-and-bailey at nearby Garpol Water. It is known the family still held the castle in the early 1300s - Roger de Kirkpatrick, Bruce's henchman of "Mak siccar" fame was described as Signeur (Lord) of Haughencas in 1306 in a document recording his loan of money to Sir Humphrey de Bohun, Earl of Hereford and Essex and Signeur of Annandale.

Kirkpatrick's stabbing of the Red Comyn in Greyfriars Monastery in Dumfries inevitably resulted in his lands being overrun and his castle occupied by the English though the family is thought to have regained possession.

It later passed to Sir Thomas Randolph, 1st Earl of Moray, Regent of Scotland during the minority of David I and companion-in-arms to Bruce and then to the powerful Douglases of Morton. It eventually became the property of the Johnstones of Corehead from whom it was acquired in more recent times by the Younger brewing family who arranged for its excavation.

Little remains today of the once proud stronghold that in medieval times controlled the route to the central lowlands. It is believed by archaeologists to have been constructed in at least two phases. Originally it took the form of a 40m x 36m quadrangular enclosure with a curtain wall, a circular tower at the north-west angle and a moat.

The castle is thought to have been demolished during the Wars of Independence and later rebuilt. Under the Douglases in the mid 15th century the walls were thickened and a crudely-built circular tower was added. In 1483 the castle featured in a notable court dispute between William Douglas and his brother-in-law Robert Maitland, a member of another powerful family.

Maitland claimed he had been granted ownership of "Auchingassil" by the Archbishop of St Andrews, and Douglas tried to force him to hand it back. Maitland appears to have won the action and in 1550 his son John succeeded to the "six merk land of Auchingassill".

John Maitland's daughter Nicolace married Sir James Douglas of Drumlanrig in 1584 but the nuptials did not bring peace to the family. In 1602 John Maitland raised an action against his son-in-law and his clerk for the murder of two Auchengassill men.

The action failed but Maitland also submitted a petition with accusations going back to 1585. It accused Douglas and the Warden of the March, a Maxwell, of twice over-running Auchengassill as part of their feud with the Johnstones. He also accused them of stealing his sheep and horses and kidnapping Maitland himself. Four years later, Sir James - ancestor of the Dukes of Buccleuch - was the owner of the castle and the Maitlands' career as a powerful family came to an end. The Buccleuchs went on to become one of the most powerful families in Kirkpatrick Juxta.

One aspect of the castle puzzled archaeologists in the 1920s - an underground passage, situated about 70 feet from the east side of the moat. It runs due north and south with the entrance apparently at the southern end and is 77 feet long by 4ft wide with a vaulted roof 7ft 9in high at the crown of the arch. H. J. Younger who wrote about it in the Journal of the Dumfries and Galloway Antiquarian Society described the passage and the chambers at each end as "baffling". He dismissed theories that it could have been an escape route, a hiding place or a sally-point and added: "It is greatly to be hoped that someone will be able to shed light on it."

More recent research has solved the mystery. According to the authors of Eastern Dumfriesshire, the 1997 report by the Royal Commission of Ancient and Historical Monuments of Scotland, the structure was a low profile emplacement for artillery and light arms. The entrance was set at 45 degrees probably to prevent flashbacks in the event of an explosion. Puzzle solved.

Beattock

Auchencass played a major role in the battles that raged throughout the Western Marches in the days of the reivers and the warring clans. It also has a place in literature: James Hogg, the Ettrick Shepherd, made the castle the residence of Willie Wilkin, the notorious Annandale warlock whose antics made his aged mother's flesh creep.

After wreaking havoc among the dead in Dumgree kirkyard and leaving his mother decapitated -

> *To Auchincastle Wilkin hied*
> *On Evan banks sae green,*
> *And lived and died like other men.*
> *For aught that could be seen.*

Highway Dramas

Although Beattock is best known for its links with the railways, the development of the road network played a key part in its history. For about 40 years, the village inn was an important staging post for mail coaches plying between Glasgow, Edinburgh and the south. Later, with the advent of the internal combustion engine Beattock straddled the busy A74 and provided services for motorists and lorry drivers. It was not until the 1960s that the village was by-passed and became the peaceful, off-the-beaten track community that it remains today.

The first properly bottomed, substantial and lasting road in the area was made, not surprisingly, by the Romans. They understood the value of good roads as an essential instrument of conquest and economic necessity. They built them expertly as direct links between their camps, fortresses and main towns. The Annandale road took hundreds of years to complete. It was started around 82 AD when Governor Gnaeus Julius Agricola began his conquest of the lands between the Solway and the Forth-Clyde line. A second phase is thought to have come towards the end of the second century when the Emperor Lucius Septimus Severus tried to re-establish control over South Scotland.

The road started at Hadrian's Wall near its west end at Stanwix, Carlisle, crossed Solway Moss, entered Scotland near the present Springfield village, and continued north by way of Birrens and Lockerbie. It then ran along the east side of the Annan, which it crossed near Beattock by an unidentified ford or bridge and continued to the Roman Camp at Milton. It passed Lochhouse Tower and proceeded along the ridge of Evan Water valley. It continued on through Chapel Farm and over Ericstane Moor and crossed the present Edinburgh Road near Auldhouse Bridge south of the Devil's Beef Tub, then carried on to the Antonine Wall between the Clyde and the Forth.

It is fairly certain that the legions advancing up Annandale would have built or repaired the road as they went, so that men and supplies could be rapidly moved up from the south. The roads were well-engineered and built on raised cambers - highways in the true sense of the word. They had a base of large cobbles or small blocks, about 160 mm across and deep, with smaller stones on top, finished with a layer of gravel. Paving stones may have been used in areas of heavy wear such as entrances to fortresses. Stones from open cast quarries and gravel from riverbeds were used in the construction and ditches were cut on either side to carry off surface water.

It is unclear whether the Roman Army maintained roads north of Hadrian's Wall after the second and third centuries AD. There is likely to have been gradual deterioration, which became even worse after the legions withdrew in 407AD. Not only were the roads abandoned with no-one to repair or maintain them but stones used in their construction were removed and used for building. The

Beattock

old Roman roads, even in their decaying state, would, however, still be used by native tribes, invading foreigners, raiding parties and travelling craftsmen.

Although it offered a high and dry route out of Annandale, the Roman highway eventually ceased to be used. Possibly the reason was sheer inconvenience for horse-riders or the boggy nature of the ground. Whatever the answer, new roads began to emerge during medieval times. One ran from Moffat to Ericstane Farm about three miles to the north where travellers could either follow the line of the old Roman road towards the Clyde or head north-eastwards by reivers' tracks into Tweeddale on the way to Edinburgh.

For the next six hundred or so years, the Ericstane Brae became the main West Coast route north. Unsurfaced from the start, it was vulnerable to erosion and travellers found it an unpleasant and hazardous route. That it survived for so long was simply because wheeled traffic was not in common use - travellers either rode, walked or, if rich, used a horse-litter. Even for mounted travellers, Ericstane Brae was not an easy route; mud and loose stone rapidly made it impassable in bad weather.

On the high plateau above Beattock stands a simple **monument** commemorating a shepherd who was killed by lightning.

Ben Wilson, of Holmshaw, was driving his lambs along the old drove road to Beattock station to join the train for Lockerbie market when he was struck down on 11 August, 1897.

His faithful collies surrounded his body and guarded it so savagely that a neighbouring herd Alec Smith, who had been helping Ben, could not get near to help.

The sandstone memorial was erected by Ben's son David who followed him as herd at Holmshaw. It originally stood on the very spot where he died but has now been moved to the side of the Crooked Road.

Highway Dramas

The road is known to have been used by William Wallace. It was also the setting for a historic meeting between Robert Bruce and James Douglas - the "Good Sir James" to the Scots and "Black Douglas" to the English. The encounter, which sealed an alliance crucial to the fate of Scotland, took place when Bruce was on his way north after killing his rival to the throne, the Red Comyn in Greyfriars' Monastery in Dumfries. The two men seem to have taken to one another on sight, and according to the poet John Barbour, who recorded the meeting, they formed an alliance that proved crucial to Scotland's fate. Douglas remained faithful to Bruce even after the King's death in 1329. Bruce's heart was removed from his body at his own deathbed request and taken by Douglas in a lead casket to the Crusades. He got only as far as Moorish Spain and just before he was killed he threw the royal heart at the enemy in defiance. It was recovered and, on the orders of his son, was buried in Melrose Abbey although Bruce's grave is in Dunfermline.

After that, the Ericstane road is mentioned only intermittently, until the period after the Restoration of Charles II when Graham of Claverhouse was hunting down the Covenanters. It was also a time when wagons were being used in the first major attempt to expand the economy. Charles II had passed laws requiring householders and landowners beside major roads to keep them in a good state of repair.

As such repairs generally came to little more than unskilled and reluctant workers tipping unsorted water-rounded stone and earth into potholes and ruts, it is hardly surprising that the road deteriorated. The surface became rutted with water-filled pools in wet weather and dried out to a surface as unpleasant to drive over as corrugated iron. Wagons could manage only 10 to 15 miles on a long summer's day - assuming they did not break down or were not toppled by boulders. Passengers were at risk of being thrown out even at low speeds.

Ericstane Brae was to have its last serious military significance when Charles Edward Stuart, Bonnie Prince Charlie, marched south past Moffat in 1745 on his abortive attempt to take the throne of England. His army brought their wagons and artillery south through the perilous route, a fearsome task even with large numbers of men available to manhandle everything down the slope.

By the 17th century stage coaches were also beginning to appear. With the horses changed at regular stages, journeys became faster but were still extremely uncomfortable and fraught with danger - from highwaymen as well as bad road conditions. Travelling along the deep-rutted, boulder-strewn dirt tracks left passengers battered and shaken. In winter weather, the risks were even greater. There are reports of coaches being stranded in snow for days and of a driver finding at his destination that his guard had frozen to death. It is said that coaching journeys were so hazardous that many gentlemen made their wills before embarking on even a relatively short trip.

Beattock

The battle to provide a proper main road from the Border to Glasgow lasted more than 50 years and was fraught with difficulties - lack of money, inadequate tolls to pay for maintenance, constant arguments between the Post Office who ran the mail coaches and the trustees who were responsible for the route, and the Government's reluctance to provide the necessary funds for construction. It took a series of Acts of Parliament to find a solution but when it finally came it ensured Beattock played an important highway role before the coming of the railways. Originally, anyone could use roads free of charge. But with the Industrial Revolution came the Turnpike Acts. Private companies called Turnpike Trusts were established and investors were given the opportunity to buy shares. The money (tolls) raised by charging people to use the roads was split between profits for shareholders and the cost of maintaining the highways.

The Ericstane Brae road was turnpiked in 1776. It was hoped the imposition of tolls taken at toll houses, or turnpikes, would yield enough money to keep the road in good repair and repay the loans taken out by trustees. The local Turnpike Trust, like others elsewhere, found, however, it could not maintain the road and it remained as bad as ever. Improvements eventually came about because of the demand for faster mail. Until the latter part of the 18th century, communications and mail between Glasgow and England were carried by mounted post boys on the treacherous Ericstane Brae. The service was not quick enough for merchants who wanted to send business orders and letters of credit or for government and other officials who needed to exchange urgent information. The post boys were also frequently attacked and robbed of their mailbags.

Entrepreneur John Palmer, the son of the owner of two Bath theatres, came up with the idea of using lightweight coaches to carry the mail, pulled by teams of horses changed at regular intervals and carrying four passengers. He prevailed upon the then prime minister William Pitt to order a trial. It proved successful and by 1785, the first fast mail coach was running between Bristol and London - the start of a nationwide network that would operate for 62 years.

The following year Palmer introduced an Edinburgh-London service and three years later Glasgow merchants persuaded the Government to run mail coaches on the Ericstane Brae route and a sum of more than £5,000 was subscribed. The Post Office, which held the monopoly on the service, at first hired privately owned coaches but later introduced its own distinctive black coaches with scarlet wheels and undercarriage. The innovation revolutionised road transport. The lightweight coaches travelled at between 7mph and 9mph, reducing the journey time between London and Glasgow from 66 to 42 hours.

It is difficult nowadays to imagine the excitement that greeted the arrival of the mail coach. The thrill is captured by the Rev W. L. McDougall who lived through the coaching era and wrote about it in an article in the Annandale newspaper.

"Coaching life was the liveliest," he wrote. "It was a great time for us youths. At first we stood aside and stared. There was the yellow, white and blue of the rattling, lumbering four-wheeler with bag and baggage on top; the four horses careering along at full speed up hill and down brae, head tossing, mouth frothing, bodies in a froth of sweat."

He went on to describe "the coachman in plush breeches, red coat and top hat and his whip with a twist, twirl and flourish". Behind was the guard in his plush red outfit tooting his horn to warn people to keep out of the way.

The inside passengers and those on top, wrapped in greatcoats, gave a passing glance as the coach flew like the wind in its race against time. Luggage was kept to a minimum so as not to reduce speed.

Anyone with a letter to mail would hand it to the guard on a pronged stick. But the mail coach did not deliver mail, which had to be picked up at the post office.

The mail coaches were popular with the travelling public but the Post Office continually threatened to withdraw the service on the Ericstane Brae route because of the state of the road. The proceeds of the tolls - which were not even paid by the mail coaches - were never enough to cover the cost of maintenance.

The need for a replacement road was so desperate that in 1798 an Act of Parliament was passed providing for the making of a new road from near Dinwoodie Green, 11 miles south of Moffat, to Elvanfoot. The preamble described the Ericstane Brae route as "incommodious and in many parts so very steep as to be impassable for wagons and other heavy carriages, inconvenient and hazardous for all wheel carriages and dangerous to travellers."

The Act provided for the appointment of groups of trustees to take charge of different sections of the new road, issue orders for construction and maintenance, for the erection of turnpikes and tollhouses and the collection of dues. They varied from eight shillings (40p) for wagons or carriages drawn by six or more horses or oxen to five shillings (25p) for coaches. Reduced charges applied to unladen horses and other animals and there were exemptions from payment for carts carrying stones for road repairs or transferring produce from one part of a farm to another, military vehicles, people going to and from church and vagrants with legal passes.

Unfortunately for the trustees, the tolls were insufficient to meet the costs of making a 100-mile stretch of road. An appeal for funds brought in more than £5,000 mainly from Glasgow merchants and public bodies and the road was completed by 1808 as far as Beattock where it ended in a cul-de-sac. Instead of carrying on south as planned, it had to turn sharply to the left two miles north of Beattock and then pass over Chapel Brae to Moffat, going south by the old Carlisle Road through Wamphray, Woodfoot and Dinwoodie Green. This half-completed route was better than the long haul over Ericstane Brae but its

Beattock

construction soon proved to be sub-standard. It could not withstand heavy traffic and bridges had not been adequately strengthened. Soon after it opened, on the stormy night of October 25, 1808, the southbound London Mail with a driver, guard, four inside passengers and two outside, sped through lashing rain down Evan Water at about 10pm. Unknown to the crew, the bridge has been partly destroyed by the rushing river and when the coach reached it there was a sudden crash. As the coach and horses plunged into the river, the lights were extinguished.

In the darkness, the only woman passenger managed to scramble out and cling to a rock in the middle of the torrent. From there she saw the lights of the northbound mail approaching and managed to attract the coachman by her screams. He drew up just in time to prevent a second disaster and in his lights saw a horrific scene. The two outside passengers were dead; the coachman, critically injured, was jammed between two rocks and the guard had suffered severe head bruising. The three inside passengers had managed to get clear of the shattered coach but were too badly injured to clamber out of the river.

The northbound crew rescued four of the victims but as John Geddes, the guard, was being lowered down the banking to bring the woman passenger to safety, modesty suddenly held him back. "Whaur will I grup her?" he shouted. "Grip me where you will so you grip me tight," screamed the beleaguered female in reply.

Help eventually arrived at the scene. The dead and injured were taken to Moffat where the ill-fated coachman died three weeks later. The Trustees could not afford to mend the broken bridge and simply fenced the gap. The coach operators had to wait seven years for a replacement.

The delay was partly due to the fact that Britain was at war with France which left little Government money available for road making. Pressure continued for improvements, however, and when the war ended with the Battle of Waterloo in 1815, a committee was formed to make a full inquiry and report. Thomas Telford, of Westerkirk, who had already been responsible for making roads through 900 miles of mountainous and boggy country in the Highlands was appointed as engineer.

The committee condemned the "most defective and ruinous state" of the road and advised that serious consideration should be given to upgrading and maintaining it. It also recommended that the State give a substantial contribution towards the estimated cost of £80,000. The following year the Government came up with £50,000 to upgrade the Evan Valley road and extend it by eight miles to Dinwoodie, cutting out the diversion over Chapel Hill. The money came with strings attached. Private subscribers had to give an equal amount and find substantial security for any excess cost. The Government also made it a condition that the Commissioners of the Highland Roads and Bridges who had done good work in opening up the Highlands should have full control of the scheme. Once the road was completed, tolls were to be used to maintain it,

Highway Dramas

THE memorial stone at Beattock Bridge recalls the connection with famous civil engineer Thomas Telford.

to pay interest on the private subscriptions and to form a fund to give investors confidence that their contributions would be repaid.

Collecting subscriptions and making the new road, much of it over boggy land, proved a massive task. The fact that an Act of Parliament was passed to allow £22,000 of the total funds to be diverted to making the road between Carlisle and Allison's Bank, Gretna, did not help. By 1829, however, the road had been improved to such an extent that the Carlisle to Glasgow Mail could cover the 94.9 miles in nine hours. But further improvements were required and in 1832 another Act was passed giving the Commissioners power to borrow so that the work could be progressed.

The extra money allowed the road to be widened and straightened and the steep hills turned into a steady gradient thanks to Telford's brilliant engineering. Telford realised the importance of good drainage. His roads were deeply dug

DESIGNED in Thomas Telford's office and built in 1822, the Beattock Inn was a premier posting house in its day.

Beattock

with large boulders at the base and two layers of smaller stones on top to make a curved surface draining into side ditches. It was an expensive but effective method of road construction.

The route of the Telford road, cutting out the treacherous track over by Chapel, helped to put Beattock on the map. Telford recommended that the junction of the new portion of the Evan Water road and the Moffat-Dumfries road was an ideal site for an inn and horse-changing post. It was midway between Lockerbie and Elvanfoot on the Carlisle-Glasgow route and was also at the intersection of that highway with the Dumfries-Edinburgh road. Telford also proposed the existing bridge should be replaced with another a short distance down stream.

As the trustees could find no-one to erect an inn or posting house at Beattock, an Act of Parliament was passed in 1821 awarding the Commissioners £5,000 to build one and find a tenant. It was designed and built in 1822 by John McDonald, a colleague of Telford, who also constructed the bridge next to it. The opening of the inn led to the closure of the King's Arms in Moffat. The Beattock establishment was large and modern with a small coach booking office on the ground floor and a spacious dining room on the ground floor for mail coach passengers. It had a reputation for high standards of accommodation, food and service and attracted some distinguished guests including Sir Walter Scott who recorded in his journal that he stayed the night there on his visit to Drumlanrig Castle in 1826. Author Oswald Mitchell, writing in 1846 about a mail coach trip, describes pulling up at Beattock Inn. He enthuses: "I see it now, the blazing fire, the smoking breakfast, the finnans and the chops and the ham and eggs, the baps and the buttered toast; how the piles kept on coming in and melting away! Surely there were never such breakfasts as the breakfasts at the Beattock Inn and never was there such picturesque travel as travel by the old mail coach."

Mitchell captures what it was like to travel by coach in his account of the Glasgow-London journey, which began punctually at 1.15am.

He writes: "The guard as he sprang into his dicky behind, gave the word to the coachman and at last, at last, we were off! Oh, the delights of it! The toot-toot of the horn and the crack of the whip as we trotted down the silent Gallowgate, the flare of our five great lamps on the hedges and the cottages and the carriers' carts, as we galloped out into the dark, the clanking and the shouting as we changed horses, and London! London! nearer with every change. I woke - but had I ever slept? - to find the sun lighting up the green Lowthers as we galloped up Clydeside, then the Summit Level, the plunge down Evan Water…"

The journey from Dumfries to Edinburgh even inspired a passenger to write a poem, recorded in Will Caesar's A Jaunt to Edinburgh, published in 1826.

The fourth verse reads:

> *The Craiglands (sic) next came in our sight*
> *The Beattock Inn is on the right*
> *Where mony a weary travelling wight*
> >   *Has gotten rest*
> *And entertainment, day and night,*
> >   *O' Wilsons' best.*

Mr and Mrs Wilson, from England, were the inn's first managers and also road trustees. In 1831, the inn stabled 50 horses, about 40 for the Wilsons' mail coach contracts and the others for posting business. The words 'Licensed to let Post Horses' - a statutory requirement - were painted on the stone archway leading to the inn yard.

Wilson was responsible for the Dumfries-Edinburgh Mail in 1831 when on February 1, a day of wild weather and falling snow, one of Scotland's worst coaching disasters took place. It is a tragic story of dedication to duty, courage, and perhaps foolhardiness. The northbound Mail with coachman John Goodfellow and guard James MacGeorge left Dumfries at 7am and headed for the Spur Inn at Moffat where, as usual, a small group of people awaited its arrival and debated whether it would continue the long, hard pull to the next stage, the inn at Tweedshaws, seven miles to the north. The general opinion was that MacGeorge "would gan on if the de'il himsel' stude across the road". Unlike the coachman, MacGeorge was a Post Office employee. An old soldier, he had a reputation as a determined man who saw it as his sacred duty to ensure the mail got through regardless of the conditions. He was spurred on by the fact that on an earlier occasion he had been reprimanded - unfairly in his opinion - for failing to weather a storm and was resolute there would be no repetition.

Against all advice, MacGeorge insisted on carrying on. He was influenced by the fact that there were only two passengers and that the total weight of the coach was not more than 30 cwts and he took the precaution of harnessing an extra pair of lead horses to be ridden octillion. As the coach plodded into the white-out, a group of men from the Spur held on to ropes attached to the roof to prevent it toppling over. Progress through the drifts was painfully slow and after three miles the coach became completely stuck. MacGeorge and Goodfellow were urged to turn back but after a hurried conference they said they would continue with the two leading horses and asked the men who had helped them to take the others back to Moffat and send a post chaise for the two women passengers, deserted in the snowbound coach. It was hours before they managed to reach them.

Meanwhile the coachman and guard then divided the mailbags between them, mounted the two horses and rode into the blizzard. James Marchbank,

Beattock

a road surveyor who had accompanied them from Moffat went with them. But after a further two miles the exhausted horses could make no further progress. MacGeorge decided to battle forward on foot, shouldering the full weight of the mailbags, some 7 stone , and Goodfellow agreed to stay with him. After trying in vain to persuade them to turn back, Marchbank left them and as darkness fell struggled through the snow towards home. He tried to lead the two horses but found it impossible and amazingly they made their own way to a farm.

The next day as the blizzard still raged, Marchbank set out with provisions to search for the two men. Just beyond the sixth milestone he found the mailbags firmly fixed to a snow post. The mountain of snow prevented him from going any further and he returned to Moffat. A search party with lanterns, spades and shovels managed to reach the Tweedshaws inn but there was no trace of MacGeorge or Goodfellow.

On the next two days more volunteers took part in further searches. Goodfellow's hat was discovered but nothing else. Then at dusk on the following day, first Goodfellow's boot and then the two bodies were found about 100 yards apart near the old road. It appeared they had been trying to take a shortcut to Tweedshaws. Goodfellow lay on his back, MacGeorge sat half erect.

Men, women and children lined the streets of Moffat for the double funeral in the old churchyard, eight days after the coach set off on its fatal journey. A hundred years later a simple cairn was erected near the spot where the men were found. It was unveiled by Sir William Younger, of Auchen Castle, who spoke of the self-sacrifice and dauntless spirit of the two "brave and loyal" heroes.

The golden days of coaching between 1830 and 1840 eventually came to an end with the advent of the railways. But even when the Caledonian Railway opened its Carlisle to Beattock section in 1843, Beattock Inn continued as a mail coach stage. Train passengers still travelled between Beattock and Glasgow by coach until the new railway line between the two points was opened in February 1848.

Although the inn lost a great deal of trade, it remained in business to cater for cross-country mail services which continued for at least 20 years.

During the tenancy of John Marshall, who was innkeeper from 1866 to 1878, the Commissioners of Highland Roads and Bridges decided to sell the inn. It was bought by William Younger, of Auchen Castle, in 1876, although Marshall's wife Jessie appears to have continued as innkeeper till she retired in 1889 when the building became the farmhouse for Lochhouse farm.

The Kirkpatrick family were tenants for 57 years before purchasing the farm from Sir Wiliam Younger, Bart in 1947. John Kirkpatrick sold the property in 1973 to Roger J. Worthy who re-opened the building as the Brig Inn and sold it to a Mr Walsh from Manchester. After a period as an old people's home, the inn

Highway Dramas

reverted to its original purpose and was bought in 1999 by Christine Harrison. At the time of writing, it is undergoing another transformation – into flats.

The Telford road remained in use for over 130 years. As the A74, it carried almost three-quarters of north-south traffic that rumbled through Beattock where the garage run by the Porteous family supplied petrol and spares. The petrol pumps at the garage, by the way, were the second to be installed in Dumfriesshire. A tea-room was added to the business in the 1920s but closed in 1939.

Maintenance of the road provided jobs for local people. Roadmen were responsible for sections along the route and took a pride in ensuring their patch was kept up to standard. Octogenarian Adam Gray, who was born at Palaceknowe, has vivid memories of seeing them as a boy.

"They were called stone nappers and their job was to break stones at the roadside," he recalled. "I used to watch them working away with their small-headed hammers with long shafts. They usually worked in pairs and were very adept at the job."

In the 1960s most of the 81-mile long A74 was upgraded to dual carriageway and Beattock was bypassed. By the early 1990s, sixty miles of the overloaded dual carriageway had been upgraded to motorway standard. North of Junction 13 (Abington) it is known as the M74 and south of that the A74 (M).

As hundreds of thousands of vehicles rush north and south along the motorway day and night, few of the occupants are aware of the existence of Beattock. Road signs and Kirkpatrick Juxta kirk overlooking the carriageway are the only clues that a village nestles nearby… changed days from the era when stagecoaches stopped at the local inn and when the call "Beattock for Moffat" resounded round the busy station platform.

Beattock's last **policeman** was Harry Erskine who served in the village in the 1960s and patrolled 56 miles of roads on his bike.

The A74 was under construction at the time and there were frequent traffic accidents - sometimes two fatal collisions in one day. Harry dealt with about 500 in five years. Shortly before his death in 2005, he recalled: "It was dangerous having to cycle along the road especially at night and I complained to my bosses in Dumfries.

"I thought they might have given me a car but no such luck. The superintendent sent me an extra tail-light for my bike. I never even bothered fitting it."

Beattock For Moffat

This is the Night Mail crossing the Border
Bringing the cheque and the postal order,
Letters for the rich, letters for the poor,
The shop at the corner, the girl next door,
Pulling up Beattock, a steady climb;
The gradient's against her but she's on time …

LOCOMOTIVES line up at the busy engine sheds during Beattock's hey-day as a rail centre.

The steady climb described by W.H.Auden in his famous poem *Night Mail* played a key role in the development of Beattock as a railway village.

Beattock Bank, as the notorious gradient is known in railway circles, is the toughest on any British main line. It is so steep - varying between 1 in 75 and 1 in 88 over 10 miles - that in the days of steam almost every northbound train required help to get to the summit, 1014 feet above sea level.

The help was provided by an assisting or banking engine, sometimes called a pilot pug, reminiscent of the children's favourite Thomas the Tank Engine.

A **"shoppers' special"** train used to run from Beattock Summit to Moffat every Saturday for the benefit of rail workers and their families whose homes were by the side of the track. It was nicknamed "The Siege" because it ran for the first time in 1900 when the Siege of Mafeking ended.

The railway families who lived along the 10-mile roadless route had no other means of getting into town for their weekend shopping. There are no stations on this section of the line but at each of the four stops the guard lowered a ladder and helped the passengers aboard. The service was withdrawn when Beattock's railway era came to an end.

A pilot pug with its two crewmen gets ready to push a train up the notorious Beattock Bank.

There were up to eight of these sturdy workhorses based at Beattock. In the early days they were usually old tender engines, retired from main line working, but by 1900 McIntosh 4-4-0s had taken over the task. They took it in turns to push the trains from behind in a long-drawn-out confrontation with gravity, then dropped off at the signal box on the summit, changed tracks and coasted back downhill.

The fleet of pugs meant Beattock was a hive of railway activity with a much larger workforce than any other country station along the line - almost 200-strong immediately after World War 2.

There was a locomotive depot and fully equipped engine sheds where engineers, fitters and cleaners carried out maintenance and repairs. There were drivers and firemen to man the locomotives, coalmen to load the fuel and gangers, lengthmen and mobile repair squads to keep the track in order. There were also supervisors, foremen, signalmen, porters, porter guards, shunters, transhippers, lampmen and signal linesmen...not forgetting the wheel-tappers.

When passenger trains stopped, a wheel-tapper would move along the coaches striking the wheels with his long-handled hammer to ensure they had no defects. Goods trains were also inspected in sidings adjacent to the main line. Many of the wagons in these days had what were called grease axle boxes

Beattock

and they often ran hot. When that happened, a defective wagon had to be taken off the train for repair or replacement.

Main line locomotives and pugs filled up with water – vital in the days of steam - at Beattock. It came from Garpol Glen, a beauty spot a mile or so north of the village and was gravity-fed to the railway station. Without this plentiful supply, the trains would never have been able to tackle the long haul up the summit.

Beattock had two signal boxes (or cabins) - north and south - manned in eight-hour shifts seven days a week. In the north box, in addition to the signalmen, there were three cabin lads who handled messages on the telegraph machine. There were also boxes at Auchen Castle, Greskine, Harthope and the Summit.

Most of the workers lived in company houses in the village although there was also a small railway settlement at the Summit. At one time, it was said that practically every Beattock family had at least one member who worked on the railway. It was not until the introduction of more powerful diesel locomotives that the pugs could be dispensed with.

One of the last of the "pug men" was the late Bob McCulloch, of Beattock, who became a fireman on the banking engines in 1941 after spells as a store boy and cleaner, "In my day, Beattock was one big railway family," he recalled. "The workers and their wives and girlfriends got together at Friday night dances and played bowls and badminton together."

There was also a railway football team in the village - the Rinky Dinks. The name is American slang for 'cheap, second-rate, outdated or unfashionable". Some of the railmen obviously had a mischievous line in humour! Their changing room was, appropriately, an old railway carriage.

Bob worked at first on Caledonian Drummond Class 2 0-4-4 pugs and later on 2-6-4 Staniers. "We pushed almost every train, passenger expresses as well as freight trains which during the war were heavily laden with iron ore and munitions. The pugs were on duty round the clock, seven days a week. It was an interesting job."

Alan G. Dunbar, a railway historian, in his book *Fifty Years of Scottish Steam* writes about the "stalwart little engines" that performed their prosaic task as bankers day in, day out..

Driving and firing them may sound monotonous, he says, but the crews did not think so - for there were compensations.

He goes on: "The job was almost within sight of home, and during the intervals of waiting at either the top or the bottom of the bank, other activities could be pursued - reading the newspaper or just having a smoke or a crack. Some of the engineers on the banking rosters spent all their railway service at Beattock and were quite content to be there. Occasionally, a little variety might come from a week or so on the Moffat branch train but the banking crews mostly worked on a shift basis that covered the 24 hours for seven days and seven nights every week."

Banking a heavy train called for a considerable degree of skill in engine driving. Passenger trains when banked were normally scheduled to take 19 or 20 minutes to cover the journey from Beattock station to the Summit, although they frequently managed it in less. Goods trains took a few minutes longer. The banking engines burned about a ton of coal on the uphill journey.

The whole operation was smart and efficient, writes Dunbar. Trains stopped at a pre-arranged point while the banking engine ran out of a siding at Beattock South Box. The slip coupling was attached by the fireman. Then the driver of the banker gave three 'crows' on the whistle - the engine in front replying in the same manner. There followed another three blasts on the banker's whistle. By this time both engines had started moving and were soon hard at work on the steep climb to the Summit where another blast on the whistle told the banker to slip the coupling. As the train pulled away at increasing speed, the banker began its easy spin back to Beattock.

Dunbar recalls some legendary tales about happenings on the bank - some patently untrue, some plausible. There was the story about a driver who carried a pail of sawdust on the footplate of the pug. The sawdust was thrown on the fire to produce a shower of sparks. Whenever the engine crew at the front looked back they could see the sparks flying out of the banker's chimney and were reassured it was pushing at full force. There were also stories of the train engine failing and the pug with Herculean effort shoving the whole cavalcade up the bank under its own steam at a spanking 30 mph.

The Galloway writer S. R. Crockett gives a nostalgic description of banking at Beattock. In his story *Beattock for Summit*, he writes: 'The drip, drip of the rain from the carriage eaves - a silence only broken by the hissing and slow panting from the engine in front - not a noisy hissing but something quiet and apologetic as if the great blue engine did not want to break some mysterious spell.

"Suddenly a bump in the rear, and one looks out and finds a noisy, squat, impudent looking tank engine has arrived behind, blowing off steam furiously and in response from three deep hoots from the giant in front, carols joyously three or four times and starts to push the train up the hill with a gay abandon that is something to see.

"Up, up through the mists until the quaintly named 'Summit Box' is reached and with a whoop from the giant in front our little travelling companion is left, after labouring so noisily and so well, left behind, straddling the rails, smug looking but withal so self satisfied but so utilitarian."

One train, however, needed no help on its long pull over the Summit - the royal train. It had two steam engines, powerful enough to conquer the gradient.

Beattock

"Two sections of line were always kept clear behind the royal train just in case anything went wrong," said ex-fireman Bob McCulloch. "All other traffic was shunted into sidings when it went past and during the war the Home Guard manned all the bridges."

The royal train, the last word in high speed luxury travel, often stopped overnight on the Beattock-Moffat branch line on its way to or from Balmoral. Villagers remember going to the side of the line to catch a glimpse of the royals.

Beattock villager Margaret Moffat recalled: "Once when I was a girl, I saw the late Queen Mother - she was Queen at the time - sitting having her breakfast when the train was stopped in the village. I remember that I felt as if I was intruding. But when people got to hear the royal train was stopped here, lots of them went to have a look. It was just curiosity."

One little girl was luckier than the rest - she had a personal audience with the King and Queen. It happened in the summer of 1947.

The late Jack Kirkpatrick, farmer at Lochhouse, Beattock - now the Brig Inn - was at home when a member of the station staff rushed up to the house and told him: "The king wants to see you."

The farmer thought it was a joke but was quickly assured it was a genuine royal summons and set off to the train, holding his five-year-old daughter Alison by the hand.

He discovered that King George VI wanted to speak to him about his herd of British Friesian cattle.

Alison now lives in New South Wales, Australia, where her husband Alister Lockhart, a Johnstonebridge man, is a farmer and Mayor of Forbes (population 8,500), a former gold rush town, famous as the place where the notorious outlaw Ben Hall was ambushed by police and gunned down in 1865. He lies buried in the town's graveyard beside Ned Kelly's sister.

Alison remembers her childhood royal occasion but admits her memories were reinforced over the years by her parents.

She said: "When I arrived at the train with my dad, the king and queen were in the field with the two princesses, Elizabeth and Margaret. There were other people from the village looking on but they were held back. We were led into the field and the king talked to my father for quite a long time. He was just very interested in the cattle. What surprised us was he knew so much about them."

She added: "My younger brother Jack had been born about a month earlier and I was just interested in telling the king that I had a new baby brother."

Alison's mother and the baby were away from home staying with friends at the time. There was a whooping cough epidemic in Beattock and she did not want to put the baby at risk.

JEANIE KIRKPATRICK remembers the day her husband and daughter met the Royals.

But, at the age of 98, she still recalled at her home on Moffat the stir caused by the royal summons - delivered, she said, by Ian Black who worked at the station.

"My husband told me he couldn't believe it when he was told the king wanted to speak to him," she said. "Afterwards the herd of cattle were known locally as the Royal Friesians - they became quite important."

The episode was also remembered by the late Jimmy Vivers, of Dumfries, one of the handpicked staff on the royal train. In a 1995 newspaper interview he told how the King and his equerry Major Michael Adeane stepped out of a carriage and went for a stroll in the field.

"The permanent way inspector was there and I remember him shouting at the pair of them 'Mind and shut the yett!' which I must say surprised me. It didn't seem the appropriate thing to say to a monarch and his right-hand man."

Jimmy, who was communications inspector on the train, added: "The king spotted the cattle and wanted to know all about them. The farmer was summoned and I remember him walking across the field with his little girl by the hand. The Queen also came out of the train that evening. She spoke to me and two of the crew and remarked on the beautiful scenery. But then she said, 'The midges are biting, I'll have to go' and she said goodbye to each of us in turn."

Trains first came to Beattock in 1847. Eleven years earlier, engineer Joseph Locke had carried out a survey for a continuation of the London-Preston railroad into Scotland. He followed the mail coach road from Beattock to the Summit and found "the ascent so steep and the countryside so rough and bleak" that he turned back and advised an alternative line from Gretna up Nithsdale to Kilmarnock. This pleased the Glasgow merchants who had already promoted two local railways linking the city with Paisley, Greenock, Ayr and Kilmarnock. The Nith Valley line was eventually opened in 1850 but in the meantime, John James Hope-Johnstone, MP for Dumfriesshire, supported by Charles Stewart, factor of Annandale estates, pressed for the Beattock Summit route. Locke surveyed it again in more detail and in 1837 gave the scheme qualified approval. Two government commissioners were appointed to investigate and after two years they gave their approval to the Annandale route.

After extensive lobbying by Hope-Johnstone and his supporters, the Caledonian Bill was given the royal assent in 1845 and the Caledonian Railway Company with its distinctive blue locomotives was formed with Hope-Johnstone as chairman.

Beattock

Despite the vast number of trains that have passed through Beattock since the line opened, there have been remarkably few serious **rail accidents** in the area.

The worst occurred on 8 June 1950 when a mother and her two children, aged four and two, another woman and a man died in a horrific fire ... caused not by a fault in the railway system but by human carelessness.

The train was the 11am Birmingham to Glasgow service, comprising 11 coaches each with eight compartments. During the journey it seems almost certain that a passenger dropped a lighted cigarette- end on the floor of one of the compartments in the second coach.

The passenger apparently got off the train at Carlisle, leaving the smouldering stub to roll under a seat and into the space formed by the floor and the wooden partition between compartments. Gradually a fire spread up the back of the partition and into the horsehair stuffing of the seats and cushions.

After about an hour, the fire had burned a hole between the sixth and seventh compartments which, like most of the others in the coach, were empty as the passengers were in the restaurant car.

When the heat shattered a window in one of the compartments, flames spurted out and ignited a cocktail of gases caused by melting paint and lacquer.

A sheet of flame roared along the corridor and into the next coach where the five passengers - who had been having tea in the compartment - were killed almost instantly.

A railway ganger Adam Moffat saw the fire as the train approached Harthope Viaduct and ran on to the line waving his arms. The train ground to a halt in seconds.

Moffat fought his way into the inferno and rescued an elderly woman who had collapsed. He returned to the carriage but was unable to stand the intense heat and thick smoke. He was awarded the British Empire Medal for bravery.

There was another fatal crash on 6 October 1971 at Murthat near Beattock where a southbound goods train sped out of control while descending the Summit. After careering through Beattock Station the engine smashed into the rear of another freight train travelling in the same direction and burst into flames. The guard's van in the second train took the full impact and the guard Robert Barbour, 52, from Bellshill, Lanarkshire, was killed.

In January 1940 the railway line was closed for three days when heavy snow with drifts of up to 20 feet blocked the Summit. The snow was cleared, loaded on to railway wagons and moved to the Moffat branch line. During the coldest winter months fires were lit around the water pipes running from Garpol Glen to stop them freezing as without water the trains could not get up the Summit.

The construction of the railway was a massive engineering job, carried out by over 7,000 navvies - short for navigators - and labourers, based in hutted camps along the route. The navvies did the blasting and cutting while the truck filling and menial jobs were left to the locally recruited casual labourers. The work was hard and relentless and called for special feats of technical ingenuity and physical endeavour to create the line over the Summit.

The Rev W. L. McDougall who watched the construction of the railway as a youth and later wrote about it in his local newspaper column recalled the navvies. "It was an eye-opener to see them at work if not at feeding time" he wrote. "They did justice to both with a will. Some took longer to steer (stir) their coffee or tea than the others but rough and ready was the order of the day"

Dressed in moleskin breeches, shovel hat and clogs with a cutty pipe for a comforter, they went forth to pick, shovel, quarry, drive or tip. The tipper was the man who, with his horse, drew a line of wagons filled with stones and tipped them one at a time over an embankment under construction. It was considered the most dangerous job.

Some of the navvies were accompanied by their wives and children and according to McDougall, the youngsters were "wild and wayward, foul of mouth and tricky in action". They had lurchers, terriers and bulldogs and spent their time rounding up wild animals. The wives, generally slovenly in dress, looked after their own huts and those of unmarried navvies.

The first navvies were the fenmen of Lincolnshire who had built sea walls and the gangs who had built roads and canals. Many also came from Scotland and Ireland and from the dales of Yorkshire and Lancashire. The Irish had a reputation as wild, hard drinking, fighting men - but it was not always justified.

The Ecclefechan-born author Thomas Carlyle wrote in 1846: "The country is greatly in a state of derangement . . .all roads and lanes overrun with drunken navvies; for our great Caledonian Railway passes in this direction and all the world here, as elsewhere, calculates on getting to heaven by steam!

"I have not in my travels seen anything uglier than the disorganic mass of labourers, sunk three-fold in brutality by the three-fold wages they are getting. The Yorkshire and Lanarkshire men, I hear, are reckoned the worst; and not without glad surprise I find the Irish are the best in point of behaviour. The postman tells me that several of the poor Irish do regularly apply to him for money drafts and send their earnings home. The English, who eat twice as much beef, consume the residue in whisky and do not trouble the postmaster."

Rioting was not uncommon. Lockerbie was said to be "quite uninhabitable" on the day, once a fortnight, when 1,000 of the workers were paid. John Baird, deputy clerk of the peace for Dumfriesshire, lamented that local boys aped the navvies - "drinking, swearing, fighting and smoking tobacco and all those sort of things."

Beattock

In April, 1846, Charles Stewart, factor of Annandale Estate, wrote to David Rankine of the railway company, telling him about the arrangements he had made with the contractors for the welfare of the workforce. A chaplain, Mr Buckeridge, was appointed at a salary of £100 plus an allowance of the same amount for his house. The contractors agreed to pay half the total and to provide a place of worship.

In his letter, now in British Transport Commission archives, Mr Stewart wrote: "For the 300 or 400 stationed at Lockerbie, being chiefly Roman Catholic Irish, it is considered best to offer education by the parish schoolmaster. It was thought that by inducing them to spend their evenings otherwise than in dissipation might tend to make them work more steadily and prevent riots.

"I engaged the parish teacher and usher for this purpose to devote two hours every evening. The men took it in grateful spirit and from 80 to 100 have been at school regularly for three months making great progress in writing and arithmetic."

Mr Stewart added: "The clergyman's chief avocation will be among the huts on Evan Water where there are or soon will be upwards of 1,000 men of the rudest class of English navvies. But south of there and in the Lockerbie district there will generally be 1,000 more who never appear at any place of worship."

The Carlisle-Beattock section of the line opened on 10 September, 1847, providing a direct link with the rapidly spreading railway network south of the border. The coming of the railway and the opening of the "first class" station designed by Andrew Heiton, of Perth, was one of the most momentous events in the history of the parish. At the opening, the trial train triumphantly steamed past the last mail coach and the occasion was celebrated with a "sumptuous collation" at the new Beattock station. For the first five months, passengers and mail arriving in Beattock at 11.16pm on the 10am from Euston and wanting to travel further north had to go by stagecoach, scheduled to reach Glasgow at 5.04am. The laying of the next part of the track over Beattock Summit involved the building of some 60 bridges and culverts and three cuttings through solid rock but the work was finished by the beginning of 1848. It is a tribute to the quality of the workmanship that the Harthope viaduct near Beattock saw service till April 2006 when it was replaced in an £8m operation to make way for 125mph trains on the line.

The "Caley" service to Glasgow and Edinburgh via Carstairs was opened in February 1848. The Post Office began to use the line the following month and the first passenger service ran in May. Express trains connecting Scotland with Manchester, Liverpool and Birmingham soon followed and the company used attractive low fares to encourage people to use the route for excursions. The banking engines came into their own. Surprisingly in the early days, engineers were less concerned with the motive force necessary to make the ascent than with the danger of trains going down the steep incline.

The problem was solved by imposing a 10mph speed limit on the downhill journey. This meant the guard had to screw on all the brakes and the driver had to run the train on the tender brakes. Sometimes if he felt he was going too slow he would put on steam and had to go into reverse to stop at Beattock Station. This led to the cracking of cylinder covers and a brake van had to be added to the trains.

When the service to the north was established, it was possible to catch the 10am train from London Euston and be in Glasgow at 1.40 the next morning - a journey of 15 hours 40 minutes. To modern travellers, it seems a long haul but in the early days of rail it was revolutionary. A timetable dated September 1849 shows that six trains ran through Beattock Station in each direction on weekdays and two on Sundays. By then the journey time from London to Glasgow had been cut to 12 hours 30 minutes.

Over the years, railwaymen in Beattock, as elsewhere in Britain, saw speeds increase by leaps and bounds - by 1890, for instance, the London-Glasgow journey time had been cut to around eight hours. The quest for speed was whetted by the famous races between the east and west coast services. In 1895, night expresses left simultaneously from London's Euston and King's Cross stations, bound for Aberdeen. The west coast train (with four engine changes en route) was the winner, covering the 540 miles in 8hrs 42 minutes, an average of 63.3mph. Its rival which switched locomotives three times averaged just over 60mph over the 523.25 miles. By the early 1900s, average speeds had risen to 80mph with locomotives reaching a maximum of 108mph. Exciting times!

In its railway heyday, Beattock was well served by trains with no fewer than seven going in each direction. The northbound 7.20am, named The Tinto after a hill near Symington in Lanarkshire, ran directly to Glasgow every weekday for the benefit of business people resident in Moffat. . It started originally at Beattock and latterly at Lockerbie and was crewed from Beattock depot.

The 3.20pm to Glasgow was called The Parly. The name stemmed from an Act of Parliament in the early days of railways, laying down that one train each way, each day should call at all stations on the route.

Most of the mail was carried on trains - Travelling Post Offices - like the one celebrated by W.H. Auden in his poetic commentary for a dramatic 1936 documentary film. The Night Mail - the West Coast Postal - swept through Beattock in the hours of darkness...

> *Past cotton-grass and moorland boulder*
> *Shovelling white steam over her shoulder,*
> *Snorting nosily as she passes*
> *Silent miles of wind-bent grasses.*

Distinguished by a row of lamps on the side of the 60-foot long coach where post office staff sorted letters at the rate of 3,000 an hour, the train collected

Beattock

BEATTOCK FOR MOFFAT

BRITISH RAILWAYS
BEATTOCK STATION ←

BEATTOCK STATION was once the busiest country station along the line.

and ejected mail en route. The mail bags in strong leather pouches, weighing between 20lb and 60lb were picked up and despatched at speed at 'catching points', using an apparatus with a manually operated extendable net fixed to the side of the carriage. The apparatus was used by the Post Office for over 100 years until it was discontinued in 1971. Beattock had a catching point just north of the bridge which carries the so-called Crooked Road over the railway line. Local mail was dropped off there and, according to older residents, was on occasion scattered far and wide when the bags burst.

In the years before and immediately after World War 2, the railways transported a lot of livestock. There were special trucks for cattle and sheep, sometimes forming a complete train particularly at the time of the lamb sales. Beattock cattle dealer Murray Jackson and local farmers regularly used the service to send cattle to shows at Crewe.

The ordinary passenger trains carried almost everything portable - from newspapers to milk in 10-gallon cans, from dogs on leads to day-old chicks and ducklings in crates, from fish in boxes to sheep and wool and a whole range of ordinary parcels and packages. Pigeon fanciers' racing birds were carried in hampers in the guard's van and released by station staff at their destination. As the homers flew back to their lofts, the time of release was marked on a special label on the hamper, which was then returned to the station of origin.

Beattock for Moffat

> Beattock railway station features in John Buchan's famous espionage thriller **The Thirty-Nine Steps** though not by name. In his desperate race to escape enemy agents, the hero Richard Hannay lands in Moffat where after dinner in a "humble public house" he walks the two miles to the junction on the main line.
>
> Hannay's narrative continues: "The night express from the south was not due till near midnight and to fill up the time, I went up on to the hillside and fell asleep, for the walk had tired me.
>
> "I all but slept too long and had to run to the station to catch the train with two minutes to spare. The feel of the hard third-class cushions and the smell of stale tobacco cheered me up wonderfully."

There is a story told about a dog which escaped from the guard's van and hared down the platform with Andra Smith, a well-known porter and local worthy, in hot pursuit, shouting: "Stop that dog, it's a parcel!"

It was the same Andra who, according to local lore, was approached by a lady who alighted from the London express and walked towards the Moffat train. "Tell me, porter," she said in a rather plummy voice. "Does this train stop at Moffat?" Quick as a flash, Andra replied: "Weel, missus, if it disna' there'll be a helluva bang!"

The single track Beattock-Moffat spur was opened in 1883 to take advantage of the increasing number of visitors from all over Britain who came to drink the waters at the elegant spa town and to enjoy the luxury of the Hydropathic Hotel opened five years earlier. The opening of the line was paid for by £16,000 raised in £10 shares.

"Beattock for Moffat" became a well-known phrase - shouted out by the porters as main line trains arrived and perpetuated by ubiquitous author R.B. Cunninghame-Graham as the title of his poignant short story about an old Moffat man travelling home by train from London to die, an expression of all the nostalgia of the emigrant Scot.

Initially, the branch line trains comprised three carriages pulled by a Drummond 0-4-4 tank engine. The railway was absorbed by the Caledonian in 1902 and was kept busy with visitors to the palatial Moffat Hydropathic Hotel until it was destroyed by fire in June 1921. In the 1930s the train gave way to

Beattock

a steam railcar known as the Moffat Bus, Puffer or Puffing Billy. It ran until around 1948 when it was replaced by an engine and coach, known as the push 'n' pull because the engine always stayed at the same end. The fare in the 1940s was 2d. one way, 3d. return, for the five-minute journey which was considered a real treat by local children.

When the Moffat-Beattock passenger service closed on December 4 1954, there were objections but they were described as "sentimental rather than insistent". Before the departure of the last train from Moffat, the town's ex-provost, businessman Robert Gunn Budge, who had used the branch line for 60 years, made an impassioned speech deploring the closure. He accused the nationalised railway executive of a gross breach of trust and bad management and suggested that, as an experiment at least, they should have run a service on the line with a light diesel engine. Before driver James O'Brien and fireman James Patterson steamed out of the station for the last time, the queen of Annandale Moira Forres laid a laurel wreath on the front of the 0-4-4T engine No. 55232 and a piper played 'Flowers of the Forest'. Among the passengers on the sentimental journey were Agnes Blyth and Thomas Tweedie who, as children, had travelled on the first Moffat-Beattock train in 1883 when champagne had been served.

When the Moffat spur was axed, Beattock was still a busy station but it had seen many changes in the previous 30 years. After World War 1, many of Britain's railway companies had been close to bankruptcy and were formed into the "Big Four" to improve management and make the railways more profitable. The Caledonian became part of the London Midland and Scottish (LMS), which continued until nationalisation in 1948 when British Railways took over the network. The second half of the 20th century saw more massive changes: passengers replaced freight as the main source of business, and the network was severely rationalised. As a result of the money-saving blueprint drawn up in 1963 by Dr Richard Beeching, chairman of the British Railways Board, about one-third of the railway system was shut down. Around 5,000 miles of track and 2,000 stations were closed.

Another big development was the replacement of steam traction by diesel and later electric power. The powerful new locomotives were able to pull passenger and freight trains up Beattock Summit unassisted, eventually bringing an end to over a century of the famous Beattock banking engines. The Beattock goods branch railway was abandoned in 1964 and the locomotive depot was officially closed on May 1, 1967 - three days after the last day of steam working in Scotland. The depot, however, was utilised for diesel stabling for 13 more years.

The new trains were faster and it was speed that led to Beattock being obliterated from the railway map. The proposal to close the station came in 1971 when four trains a day in each direction still called there. The Railways

Board stated that with completion of the electrification of the West Coast main line it was intended to introduce very fast inter-city services, which necessitated the severe restriction of the number of stops. Lockerbie was to be retained as the main railhead for the area and, it was stated, a further stop at Beattock would add five minutes to journey times to every inter-city train calling there. If the station was retained, it was argued, it would cost £12,000 to lengthen the platform and build a new over-bridge. Closure on the other hand would mean a saving of £4,000. Although Beattock Station generated £6,000 in 1970, the Railways Board claimed not all of this would be lost as people would still travel by rail.

News of the proposed closure was greeted with anger. A public meeting was held in Moffat and a petition and a Save Our Services campaign was launched. The campaign had the support of Beattock Community Council, Moffat Town Council, Dumfries County Council, Moffat Merchants and Traders Association, the principals of the town's three private schools and the Scottish Railway Development Society. There was a total of 83 formal objections, 73 of them from individuals.

Moffat Town Hall was packed to capacity for the inquiry by the Transport Consultative Committee for Scotland into the proposed closure. Moffat town clerk Hugh Simpson made the main statement, basing his objection on present and future hardship, especially to elderly retired people on fixed incomes, the 200 private school pupils and local students who had to travel to Glasgow or Edinburgh. He listed some special cases - a grocer who would no longer be able to receive quick delivery of "continental perishables" from London by passenger train, and newsagents who would not be able get their English daily papers.

Mr Simpson dealt in detail with local bus services which he said provided inadequate connections for people wanting to travel by train from Dumfries and Lockerbie, respectively 20 and 16 miles distant.

He asked: "For how much longer will British Railways be permitted to exercise a policy which results in rural areas becoming depopulated while the heavily populated areas become even vaster, giving rise to all the social ailments so prevalent in cities in Britain since the war?"

Dumfries MP, the late Hector (later Lord) Monro told the inquiry the closure would affect about 4,000 people. But Andrew McKay, assistant general manager of British Railway's Scottish region said the number of people using the station over the previous 10 years had sharply declined - from 8,200 in 1960 to 3,400 in 1970. An average of only 10 passengers boarded the eight trains at Beattock each day and about the same number alighted there, he said, and only three people used the station regularly. He said the banking engines had been reduced and would disappear almost entirely with electrification which had already begun.

Beattock

It took six months for the decision on the station's future to be announced and when it came it was disappointing. It was reported that the Consultative Committee considered that hardship would be experienced by only a limited number of station users. They suggested it would be alleviated if local bus services were accelerated and slightly re-routed.

The Environment Secretary Peter Walker, who had the final say, ruled that the station must be axed. It was closed to passengers on New Year's Day, 1972, and closed completely in 1983. It was the end of the line for "Beattock for Moffat". The dignified station with its crow-stepped gable and its once busy bookstall and buffet was demolished followed by the locomotive shed, leaving little evidence of a piece of railway history stretching back to the middle of the 19th century. Northbound trains now take the bank easily in their stride, so different from the 'romantic' days of steam.

At the time of writing, Beattock's former sidings are being used as a freight terminal and there are moves to reopen Beattock Station for local passenger services. The future is in the hands of the politicians and the railway authorities.

• One Beattock man rose from the position of booking clerk at the village station to be chief executive officer of the LMS in Scotland. John Ballantyne was born at Greenhill Cottage in Palaceknowe and died in his 70s in 1951.

A TRAIN arrives in Beattock Station in the days when it was still a busy stop on the main London-Glasgow line.

Kirks, Ministers and Ghosts

Kirkpatrick Juxta may sound an odd name for a parish. Juxta is Latin for 'near' or 'close to' and it was so-called to indicate it was closer to the bishop's seat in Glasgow than the parishes of Kirkpatrick Durham, Kirkpatrick Fleming and Kirkpatrick Irongray.

Until the 15th century, it was called simply Kirkpatrick after St Patrick, the famous Romano-British missionary who was sent by Pope Celestine I to Ireland in the 5th century and spent 40 years there spreading the Gospel.

The first known mention of the name 'Kirkpatrik Juxta' was in 1355 in the Queensberry papers but very little is known of the early parish. Much of the history of the medieval church in Scotland is shrouded in mystery, partly because the country had no metropolitan authority - no archbishop. From the early 12th century, successive popes ordered the Scottish bishops to owe obedience to the Archbishop of York - a direction that was scrupulously ignored for nearly 100 years. The Scottish bishops had therefore to be consecrated by the Pope himself or by a papal legate. The independence of the Scottish bishops was finally established in 1189 when a papal bull ordered that every Scottish diocese (except Galloway) had to answer to the Pope directly. This meant that a vast deposit of records relating to the everyday life of the Church in Scotland was stored not locally but in Vatican archives.

Like other parts of Scotland that had been evangelised by Ninian, Columba or Mungo, Annandale would have had its simple places of worship in early medieval times but little trace of them remains - hardly surprising as the countryside was regularly ravaged and almost every building razed.

One of the first known references to a church in Kirkpatrick Juxta occurs in the 12th century. Records show that Robert de Brus, Lord of Annandale and ancestor of King Robert the Bruce, reached an agreement with Engelram, Bishop of Glasgow (1174-84) to cede the patronage of the church at Kirkpatrick Juxta to the Bishops of Glasgow. This was endorsed by Engelram's successor Jocelyn, confirmed by the pope in 1216 and continued till the Reformation.

There was also a church at Dumgree, about four miles south-west of Beattock, dating to the same period. Only the foundations still exist, surrounded by a graveyard with the remains of tombstones. Dumgree (also known as Drumgreioch) was originally a parish in its own right but it was split between Kirkpatrick Juxta and Johnstone and the church ended up in Kirkpatrick Juxta.

Dumgree kirk is known to have been in existence around 1180 when Walter de Carnato, a landowner of Norman descent, granted the parsonage teinds (one-tenth of the income from the land) to the Abbot of Kelso, a gift confirmed by Walter, Bishop of Glasgow.

Beattock

The site of this ancient building is on the farmlands of Parks. The farmer's wife Margaret Thorburn remembers years ago when it was fenced off but now it is unprotected and cattle and sheep graze over it.

"The gravestones are broken and lying face down," she said. "We sometimes get people coming here to look for their ancestors' graves. Recently a family from America called Brown spent a whole day in the kirkyard looking for the grave of a relative who had been buried there in the 17th century. They found it after turning over some of the old flattened tombstones. It is a pity the place could not be excavated and researched."

Another early church could have been located on the north-east shoulder of Peat Hill adjacent to Kinnelhead farm, about four miles west of Beattock. The Inventory of Monuments in Dumfriesshire describes a ruinous structure built into the rock with a vaulted roof and at least one other storey. The fact that it is bigger than the usual domestic or domestic-and-defensive building, and the presence of three crosses carved in the rock "would seem to suggest an ecclesiastic purpose". One of the crosses is above the main doorway and the others on nearby rocks. It has proved difficult to date them but it is thought most likely that they are from the late medieval period

From this time onwards records of Kirkpatrick Juxta Church are more plentiful. One dating from 1489 concerns a court action heard by the Lord Auditors in Parliament. It was brought by the parson Clement Fairlie, against several people who had robbed him of the Easter offerings and the penny offerings of St Patrick's Day, amounting to 10 merks, and had stolen 200 lambs valued at £18 and a sack with 24 stones of tithe wool worth £12. He also accused them of unjustly possessing and working land belonging to the kirk. The Lords ordained the defenders to make full restitution and pay damages.

The Kirkpatrick Juxta parish records provide some interesting glimpses of post-Reformation church life and reflect the range of duties undertaken by the kirk session. Apart from overseeing arrangements for conducting christenings, marriages and funerals, they administered discipline, rebuked and censured, admitted and expelled members, took charge of the poor and looked after education. They were, in effect, the local authority in their respective parishes.

Some ministers were stricter than others. The Rev Thomas Goldie, son of a Moffat schoolmaster, who became minister in 1692, cited no fewer than 17 members of the congregation to appear for various offences at his first session. A month later, William Wilken, of Red Brae, was summoned for Sabbath breaking - a charge he denied. But a witness, Andrew Gillespie, testified that he had seen Wilken lifting peats on a Sunday about a month earlier. But he claimed he had been lifting only a piece of mossy turf to put under the girding of his horse that had a sore back. Other witnesses were called and the case dragged on for 18 months until it was finally brought to an end by Wilken's death. The story begs the question: how much did the kirk inquisition contribute to the demise of the unfortunate accused?

From 1567, there is a fairly complete list of the ministers of Kirkpatrick Juxta, starting with Mungo Niven who served from 1567 till 1580. He was followed by John Colquhoun, described as "parson", in the early part of the 17th century. The next to be named was George Buchanan in 1626 when a church and manse were built. He was transferred 11 years later to Moffat, the home town of his successor the Rev David Wauche (or Waugh) who served until his death in 1653.

The next two ministers became caught up in the turmoil of Covenanting times when around 400 ministers - fully one-third of the clergy of the Church of Scotland - were driven out of their churches, manses and deprived of their stipends. James Porter was kicked out of his office for holding Conventicles (clandestine field services) and Robert Murchiston suffered a similar fate for refusing to "take the test" - in other words refusing to renounce Presbyterianism in favour of Episcopacy - but he was later received back into communion.

He was succeeded by Archibald Ferguson who was ousted by a rabble of men and women who beat him and tore off his clothes in front of his wife - although the records do not say why.

The next two ministers, Thomas Goldie and William Scott, had less hectic terms of office but had the distinction of serving the parish for the longest periods in its history – 42 years and 50 years respectively. William Scott was succeeded by his son Gabriel who after 12 years was followed by William Singer, arguably the most distinguished minister in Kirkpatrick Juxta's long history. Transferred from Wamphray in 1799, he served for 41 years, became a doctor of divinity in 1808 and Moderator of the General Assembly in 1830. A great agriculturist, he wrote authoritative books and articles on the subject and was author of the chapter on Kirkpatrick Juxta parish in the 1834 Statistical Account of Scotland.

He died in 1840 and was succeeded by William Little who earned a reputation for his knowledge of natural history. He corresponded with the leading entomologists of his day and contributed articles to the Magazine of Zoology and Botany. He was also a prizewinner and judge at Moffat Horticultural Society. His successor, Robert Colvin, who rebuilt and enlarged the manse was followed by William Brodie, William Finlayson (minister throughout War 1) and James Fordyce (who served during World War 2). Five ministers were in post in the years from the end of the war to the millennium - Frederick Tidd, Thomas Nichol, Charles Cooper, Ian Ramsay and Jack Stewart. The parish was linked with Wamphray and St Andrew's, Moffat, in 2001 and all are served by one minister - David McKay, at the time of writing.

The present Kirkpatrick Juxta church was built between 1798 and 1800 at a cost of £230 1s 10d on the site of an earlier kirk, a low thatched building, dating from 1626. The new church was designed by a Dumfries mason, John McCracken, and built of whin rubble with red sandstone dressings. It was

Beattock

KIRKPATRICK JUXTA CHURCH, opened in 1800 and remodelled 75 years later, is a local landmark.

remodelled in 1875-7 by Dumfries architect James Barbour who provided new windows, including two large roses, heightened the gables and replaced the West or Bride's Door with a new main door commanding a panoramic view of Moffat and its beautiful hills and valleys. The roof was re-slated with best "London Lancashire slates" and the finest materials were used throughout the building. The interior is all Barbour's including the impressive vaulted timber ceiling constructed with best Baltic pitch pine timbers.

The church has been fortunate in receiving many memorial gifts over the years - a fine communion table, lectern, bible, brass offertory plates, flower stands and other items still in use. The organ was presented by Bertram Smith's wife. In the vestry are mementoes from an earlier age - a pewter collection plate, communion tokens, collection ladles and a crocheted copy of the Lord's Prayer. Friends from Los Angeles gifted the kirk a book of sermons preached there during the 1700s.

HEADSTONES in the parish kirkyard date back to 1685 and have some interesting stories to tell.

Like all ancient kirkyards, Kirkpatrick Juxta's has some interesting headstones. The oldest, dating back to 1685, was erected to the memory of Lilias Proudfoot, of Annanholm.

Another ancient stone commemorates James Johnstone, of Bierholm (descendant of Lord Warriston) who died in 1739. According to local tradition, it was originally attached to the wall of the previous church.

A memorial to the Alston family bears the figures of four children and the motto: "By hammer in hand all arts do stand". On the reverse is an inscription:

> *Ingenious Alston from this world is gone*
> *From a dunghill to sit upon a throne*
> *In highest heaven here now aloud he sings*
> *Eternal praises to the King of Kings.*

Another quaint inscription for an 85-year-old who died in 1734 reads:

> *Here lies John Waugh*
> *Whom death did call*
> *From a vain world*
> *And that is all.*

The old Dumgree kirkyard also has some interesting headstones, most of them sadly toppled and damaged. Among them was one standing higher than the others. It marks the grave of a Johnstone who was determined his body would never be stolen in a Burke and Hare-style raid. He ordered his wooden coffin to be encased in two others - one of lead and the outer one of stone. Not only that: the stone coffin was securely bolted to the ground.

According to a local tradition the witches of Annandale used to meet in the old churchyard. H. Drummond Gauld waxes lyrical about the legend in his 1934 book Brave Borderland.

"On stormy night when the moon was full and winds boomed in the glens," he writes, "the affrighted peasant folks would tell of strange visions in the scudding clouds high athwart the glimmer of the moon and of shriekings and clattering broomsticks in the old kirkyard of Dumgree."

The graveyard also contains a huge stone called Willie Wilkin's Craig - named after a famous warlock who had a reputation for conducting devilish orgies. The story goes that when Willie Wilkin was on his deathbed, he charged his sons, as they valued their peace and prosperity, to sing no requiem or pronounce any burial service over his body but to put a strong withie (rod) at each end of his coffin and carry him away to Dumgree. There, they were to lay it on a stone and rest a few minutes and if nothing happened proceed with the burial. If they fulfilled these commands, Willie promised them the greatest happiness and prosperity for four generations. But if they neglected them in any detail, they would suffer the utmost misery and wretchedness.

Beattock

The lads performed everything according to their father's directions but had no sooner set down the coffin than they were alarmed by the most horrible bellowing. Suddenly, Satan's twin bulls appeared roaring and snuffing and tossing up the earth with their horns and hooves. When they reached the coffin they lifted it with their horns and ran off with it towards the west. Those mourners who were on horseback gave chase but when they came to Loch Ettrick near Closeburn the bulls with a roar like thunder plunged into the depths of the water with the coffin and were never seen again.

Willie was reputed to be keen on curling and according to the legend he and his hellish confederates continued to play the game on the loch during the long winter nights.

Dumgree is reputed to have a ghost, The Grey Lady, who stalks the old kirkyard. According to one version of the tale, the mistress at Stidriggs, about a mile and a half to the north, was worried about her son's nocturnal wanderings and suspected he was surreptitiously seeing a girl. One night she saddled her horse and went in search of the errant lad. Reaching the church, she saw it was lit up and peered in a window. To her astonishment, she saw the boy in a group performing satanic rituals. When she cried out, they set upon her and killed both her and her son to prevent their terrible secret being revealed.

The Soldier Monks

Interest in the Knights Templar, the military and religious brotherhood who dominated medieval Europe, has been revived by Dan Brown's best selling and highly controversial novel *The Da Vinci Code*.

The book, which has spawned many others on the subject, associates the Templars with Rosslyn Chapel near Edinburgh but they also had links with other parts of Scotland including, it appears, Kirkpatrick Juxta.

The knights were great landowners, farmers and traders and their holdings in the area are thought to have been extensive with a church, living accommodation and possibly a hospital.

Today, the only remaining physical link with them in the area is the sparse ruin of a 13th century chapel, partly built into a house on Chapel Farm. It is listed by Simon Brighton as a Templar site in his book *In Search of the Knights Templar*.

The Order, which left a legacy that has spanned the centuries, was founded in about 1119 to protect the Holy Land and to safeguard Christian pilgrims. The idea of a band of knights subject both to military discipline and monastic oaths was probably the brain-child of a knight from Champagne, Hugh of Payens, who persuaded Baldwin I, King of Jerusalem, to allow him to install himself and a few companions in a wing of the royal palace, a former mosque in the Temple area.

Kirks, Ministers and Ghosts

THIS is all that remains of a 13th century chapel linked to the Knights Templars at Chapel Farm near Beattock.

The Order had three classes: knights, all of noble birth; sergeants, drawn from the bourgeoisie, who were the grooms and stewards of the community, and clerics who were chaplains and in charge of non-military tasks. The Templars' badge was a red cross worn on a white tunic by the knights and on a black tunic by the sergeants.

The Order had the patronage of the Pope and was championed by Bernard of Clairvaux, founder of the Cistercians. They owned extensive property in Europe and the Middle East and were empowered to levy taxes and tithes on the lands they controlled. They introduced banking to Europe.

The Templars and the Order of St John which provided hospitals for the pilgrims are said to have been introduced to Scotland by King David I (1124-53) who is believed to have given them their first grants of land.

Typical of Templar foundations, St Cuthbert's in Kirkpatrick Juxta owned valuable land but it is not known how many knights or sergeants were based there or how many, if any, travelled from this part of Scotland to the Holy Land. There were, however, links between Annandale and the Crusades. It is estimated that of the 5,000 men led by the Earl of Huntingdon to assist King Richard Coeur-de-Lion in the Third Crusade, 1000 belonged to Annandale and most of those were Hallidays.

After two centuries, the white knights were disbanded, victims of their own success. Their huge financial and military power and unique privileged position brought them into conflict with other sections of the Church including the rival Order of St John and they were accused of corruption and heresy. These accusations, still a subject of controversy, and the greed of King Philip the Fair of France who wanted to grab their banking organisation and network meant inevitable ruin. On Friday, October 13, 1307, many were arrested, tortured and executed. In 1312 Pope Clement V issued a Papal Bull disbanding the Templars.

Exactly what became of St Cuthbert's at this time is not known but it would seem that remnants of the Order remained in Scotland where Robert the Bruce - excommunicated for murdering Red Comyn - is said to have supported it. It has been speculated that a division of Knights Templars fought on the side of the Scots at Bannockburn and helped to rout the English although there is no evidence for this.

Whatever the truth about the fate of the Scottish Templars, it is known that the barony of St Cuthbert was acquired around 1500 by a branch of the French family who had owned land in the area since the 12th century.

All The Stats

A fascinating window on Kirkpatrick Juxta in a bygone age is provided in the three Statistical Accounts of Scotland. They may look like musty old tomes but they provide an accurate and revealing picture of every parish in the country over a period of almost two centuries. The first two provide vitally important reference sources for a critical half century spanning the Agricultural and Industrial Revolutions.

The *Old* or *First Statistical Account* was launched in the 18th century under the direction of Sir John Sinclair of Ulbster (1754-1835), MP for Caithness. Known as 'Agricultural Sir John', he conceived a plan to ask parish ministers of the Church of Scotland all over the country to reply to a set of planned questions dealing with subjects such as the geography, climate, natural resources and social customs of each parish. His stated aim in 1790 was "to elucidate the Natural History and Political State of Scotland" and he later defined the accounts as: "an inquiry into the state of the country for the purpose of ascertaining the quantum of happiness enjoyed by its inhabitants and the means of its future improvement."

The returns from the parishes were published when they were received in a series of twenty-one volumes between 1791 and 1799.

The article on Kirkpatrick Juxta was the work of the Rev Gabriel Scott who described the parish in rather unflattering terms. "The general appearance is rather bleak, interspersed with moss and moor and almost without enclosures," he wrote.

He records that the population had decreased over the previous half century and in his time it stood at 617 - 298 males and 319 females. They ranged from 156 children under 10 to two adults aged over 90. The 132 houses in the parish accommodated at least five people each.

Everyone could read pretty well and all the men could write. "Several of the farmers read history, magazines and newspapers," wrote Scott. "The vulgar read almost nothing but books on religious subjects. Many of them are too fond of controversial divinity - a taste which the Dissenters (opponents of the established church) are very diligent in promoting…"

The first legal school in the parish had been opened only 20 years before the report was written and "the number of scholars in summer is very small and in winter 40 or 50". The dominie received only £11 a year (compared with the minister's stipend of over £72 plus a glebe worth £4 10s a year). Scott commented: "Had not the present teacher been disabled for working as a common mason, he must have spurned at such a livelihood as this."

Small as the salary was, it appeared to be slightly above the average earnings for an unskilled worker in Kirkpatrick Juxta at the time.

Beattock

Scott gives the example of a labourer with a wife and four children aged between 5 and 13. He would have earned £10 6s 8d (including his children's wages of £1 and charity or presents of 10s). His income, probably augmented by his wife's harvest work or spinning, was barely enough to cover the family's annual outgoings. A servant's wages were even lower - £6 to £8 for a man and between £2 10s and £4 for a woman. Yet despite the low wages many families seemed to survive without charity.

"The people in general are quiet, sober and contented," writes the minister. "No murder, suicide or robbery is known to have happened in the parish. Almost every family spins coarse cloth for its own use but unfortunately there is no considerable woollen manufacture in Annandale. Fifty years ago, silk and cotton were very rarely to be seen; now a servant maid cannot be in dress without both."

Listing other signs of progress, Scott says that half a century before his time "there were then no watches but the minister's; now there is scarcely a man servant who is without one. Clocks, mostly of wood, are also very common."

Windows were another innovation. Seventy years earlier only two houses had glass panes but "now every house has at least one glass window".

On health, Scott reports that the common people "are strongly prejudiced against inoculation for smallpox" (a very recent and radical concept) and adds: "To this circumstance a large proportion of the deaths in the parish is to be ascribed." Rheumatism, he adds, is much more common than it was 40 years earlier. "I have heard no satisfactory reasons assigned for its increase," he states. "Thinner clothing and the more general use of linen next the skin may perhaps account for it in part."

Fast forward to the *New* (or *Second*) *Statistical Account* that was mostly written in the 1830s and issued in 1845. The article on Kirkpatrick Juxta was the work of the Rev Dr William Singer, a distinguished minister who served in the parish for 41 years, was Moderator of the General Assembly in 1830 and also a noted agriculturist and writer. His best known book *A General View of Agriculture in Dumfriesshire* was published in 1812.

Writing in 1834, he records that the population of the parish had risen by almost 60 per cent in just over 40 years - from 617 in 1790 to 981 in 1831. In his time there were 169 families with an average of five children. The population of Beattock village was about 80. Seventy-three families were employed in agriculture and 40 in trade, manufacture and handicraft. Income had also gone up during this period. In the 1830s, a man's day wages in summer were 1s 6p (about 7.5p) and 2d or 4d less in winter. This equates to about £20 a year (double the 1790 figure). A tradesman received about one-third more. But farm-servants' wages were still at the lowest end of the scale - £10 to £12 a year for men and £6 to £7 for women.

All The Stats

By present-day standards, of course, food and other commodities were cheap. A canny household would have got 4s (20p) change out of £1 after buying 1 cwt of coal (delivered), a cart load of peats (delivered), a cubic foot of larch timber, 1lb of butter, 1lb of cheese, 1lb of beef or mutton and a stone of coarse wool.

Surprisingly there were no fewer than seven schools in the parish in Singer's day with a total roll of more than 200 children. Two of them were parochial schools, two were fee-paying (with fees ranging from £15 to £20 a year) and the others are described as "inferior". The salary of the first parish schoolmaster was £34 4s 4d (three times more than 30 years earlier) while the master at the second school who appears not to have had a permanent contract received only half that amount. The minister's stipend totalled £228 plus £10 income from the glebe - more than six times the schoolmaster's salary.

Not surprisingly, low wages and big families resulted in poverty. Although there were only between 8 and 12 on the poor list, receiving just over £4 a year, there were many others needing incidental aid for themselves and their children. The church which had about 380 communicants at this time collected about £30 a year and also received voluntary contributions to help the poor.

THE former primary school in Beattock had about 80 pupils, about double the present roll.

Beattock

Singer obviously felt strongly about the issue of poverty. "The great evil of the poor system in Scotland arises out of uninterrupted public begging," he wrote. "There is no remedy but one, namely, to enforce residence in the parishes where the poor are known, and where they must work, and will be looked after.

"If residence were enforced everywhere and settlements not acquired so easily, the poor laws of Scotland would be almost perfect and neglect of the poor would cease where it now exists."

Referring to the 1834 Poor Law "passed for clearing England of vagrants from Scotland and Ireland" he argues that Scotland needs similar legislation to protect it from English vagrants and "the hordes that infest it from Ireland". He was obviously writing before the days of political correctness!

When Singer contributed his article, Britain was at peace and fairly prosperous but he casts his mind back to the early years of the century when the country was at war with France.

He writes: "In 1803, when a volunteer force was of such eminent service for the peace and defence of the kingdom, this parish met for prayer and conference and offered one man for every eight persons of the whole population to serve

---

Kirkpatrick Juxta once had its own **hospital** - but only for a few months.

The Emergency Hospital at Middlegill to the north of Beattock was erected to deal with an outbreak of diphtheria in the Evan Valley in 1901 - almost 40 years before there was an effective vaccine for the disease. The outbreak was caused, according to a report by the medical officer of health, by unsanitary conditions at the school toilets.

The first three cases proved fatal and when it became impossible to isolate and nurse new cases in their own homes, the health authorities put up the temporary hospital comprising a steel building, a military hospital marquee and a bell-tent as a disinfecting station at a cost of £250. It was staffed by three nurses who were provided with sleeping accommodation in a neighbouring cottage. Twenty-nine diphtheria cases were treated in the hospital, which was in use till the beginning of September.

as volunteers in arms, about 80 holding up their arms to give this pledge, and with hardly any distinction between church-going people and dissenters."

This was 20 more than the neighbouring parishes of Wamphray and Johnstone and obviously a source of local pride.

"The Minister for Scotland, the late Lord Melville, had foreseen this happy result; and the venerated monarch (George III) happily authorised that important and salutary measure (the creation of a volunteer force) which prevented invasion as well as disturbance," added Singer.

More than 100 years passed before the *Third Statistical Account* appeared in 1962. Sheila G. Forman, of Craigielands, wrote the article on Kirkpatrick Juxta in 1951 and revised it seven years later. It brings up to date the parish population figures which reached a peak of 1,097 in 1851 then dropped again to 980 in 1901, rose to 1,021 in 1921 and fell again to 878 in 1951.

By then the population of Beattock village was about 300.

By this time, the parish's social life was very active, she reports. Carpet bowling, football, curling and badminton clubs flourished and there were playing fields with a football pitch, children's play area and youth club providing classes in choral singing, drama, Scottish country dancing, dressmaking and leatherwork. Other bodies included the Women's Guild, Girl Guides and WRI with about 100 members.

"In spite of the wireless and television, the cinema in Moffat and the centralisation of many aspects of daily life, the parish is keenly interested in its own social welfare and entertainment and is proud of its long-standing reputation for independence," declared Forman.

But some of the old traditional events had ceased to be held. Beattock Show had come to an end in 1934 and the sheepdog trials were abandoned two years later.

The inn and two licensed alehouses mentioned by Singer no longer existed in the 1950s. The Moffat weekly market had also been abolished and farmers went instead to Lockerbie and Dumfries.

Of other changes, she writes: "Many of the old sayings and customs of the countryside have now died out and members of the present generation seldom quote the proverbs or use the expressions of their grandfathers' time. Neither are the old traditions followed today: not even the Fast Day (the Thursday before each of the twice yearly communion Sabbaths) has been observed for a number of years."

"Over the years," adds the perceptive Miss Forman, "the parish has tended to become less isolated, less rural and more social and it is now more closely connected with the outside world, mainly because of the coming of rail and road transport, the generally improved living conditions and the standardisation of life in all sorts of ways. There is no doubt that the working classes in the parish have a much better way of living than their forefathers, with more money to

Beattock

THE names of the dead of two world wars appear on the
Kirkpatrick Juxta war memorial.

All The Stats

spend, more luxuries to enjoy, better transport, free education for the children and plenty of amusement and recreation."

In her time there were no poor in the parish and generally speaking everyone was well and decently dressed. The agricultural worker in particular has benefited by the introduction of machinery, shorter hours and higher wages. Other classes, however, she pointed out, tended to be worse off financially owing to death duties and higher taxation."

Writing during the Cold War, she echoes the feelings of the time when she adds: "Another side of the picture is the universal lack of security and contentment brought about by this atomic age and by the inward fear of war felt by all those who have already been through the World Wars."

While the rest of the country celebrates **Hallowe'en** on October 31 - the eve of All Saints Day - Beattock marks the spooky night on November 11.

The switch of date has been attributed to a change in the calendar in the 18th century. Older generations in Beattock claim their unique Hallowe'en date is "old style".

The original Roman calendar was based on a year of 365 days but in the time of Julius Caesar it was discovered that the actual length of time taken for the earth to orbit the sun was nearer to 365.25 days and in the Julian calendar an extra day was added every four years. But this calculation was a slight over-estimate and by the 16th century a cumulative error had occurred. To correct this, Pope Gregory XIII removed 10 days from the calendar in 1582 by decreeing the day following October 4 would be October 15. and by adjusting the arrangements for leap years. Not all countries accepted this change and it was not adopted in Scotland till 1752. By this time the error had increased to 11 days because of a dispute over whether 1700 was a leap year. An Act of Parliament decreed that September 2 would be followed by September 14, expunging the 11 days in between.

Anyone refusing to go along with the new style would therefore retain the 11 lost days. This meant October 31 would be, for them, November 11.

The Big Hoose

CRAIGIELANDS HOUSE, a Grecian-style mansion built for brewer William Younger, once played a big part in the life of the community.

To generations of Beattock residents, Craigielands was "the big hoose". Although it was a world away from ordinary village life, it was closely integrated with the community. Many locals were employed in the mansion and on the estate and home farm; curlers enjoyed bonspiels on the man-made lake; barbers and tutors called regularly and tenants' children were invited to Hallowe'en and Christmas parties. The Craigielands Curling Club, formed in 1834, provided one of the main sporting opportunities in the winter months.

The elegant villa and its two lodges were designed in Greek revival style by distinguished Edinburgh architect William Burn. It was his first known wholly Grecian house and became a model for many other middle-sized Scottish mansions. It was built for the brewer William Younger in 1817 and was later owned by William Colvin, a Glasgow merchant who presented the town of Moffat with its landmark ram statue and fountain in 1875. Seven years after that, Craigielands was bought by James Smith, prosperous partner in a Liverpool firm of cotton spinners and brokers. At first he used it as a weekend retreat but later in his life he spent up to half the year there. He extended the house, enlarged the stables, built modern cottages for tenants, stocked the lake with trout, opened a hatchery to populate the River Annan and the hill burns, designed

The Big Hoose

and planted coverts for peasant shooting, created the curling rinks and in 1884 started the curling club which hosted a Scotland-England match in 1902.

Thanks to James Smith's grandson, Sir Denis Forman, who was born at Craigielands in October 1917, and spent much of his childhood there, we have a detailed picture of the house and the upstairs, downstairs life of the family and staff in the early years of the 20th century. Forman's book *Son of Adam*, published in 1990, is an account of his rite of passage from childhood to teenage years and the germination of his two main interests: entertaining an audience and music. His main influences were his Edinburgh-born grandmother, a pious disciplinarian whose "authority was absolute" and his eccentric father and uncles, all old boys of Loretto, the independent and rather unconventional Edinburgh boarding school. The main theme of the story is his rejection of the beliefs and values of his elders, especially their conventional Christian religiosity that he rejected in favour of rational atheism, leading to a showdown with his family at the age of 15.

But his view of Craigielands remained constant. He loved the Palladian mansion with a passion and describes it in almost poetic terms – set against the background of a high wooded escarpment and when viewed from the other side of the valley "standing out like a white ship on a dark sea".

Forman tells of life in the nursery and on the estate with its farm, stables, kennels, laundry and sawmill and introduces readers to the range of workers and villagers who came into contact with his extended family.

Their faults and idiosyncrasies are not spared as he scans them in his frank and uncompromising style with a sharp eye for detail. One nurse breathes halitosis "like a dragon breathes fire", a cook "could not cook at all", one tablemaid had a stammer "approaching a state of lockjaw", another was an over-plump lumpkin of a girl and the head gardener was "patronising and a bore". The village schoolmaster John Bulman, who tutored Forman for a time, comes in for some of the most stinging criticism. He is described as a "small, ferret-faced Welshman with a furtive look and a twitch at one corner of his mouth" and condemned as being able to teach nothing beyond elementary school standard. Bulman was secretary of the local agricultural show and, according to Forman, "was regularly drunk by four o'clock on a show day" and fell from grace after small sums of money went missing. The local minister at the time, W. L. Finlayson, does not escape the writer's scorn. He is dismissed as "a pitiable soul" whose style of ministry had driven the Smith family to worship in Moffat rather than in Kirkpatrick Juxta Church and who eventually committed suicide by wandering into the path of a train. Beattock people who remember the teacher and the minister view them more sympathetically and resent the way they and others have been maligned in the book. In Forman's defence, it has to be said he was remembering characters as he saw them through the eyes of a young boy and at a time when he was rebelling against the lifestyle at Craigielands.

Beattock

The mansion was bought in 1948 by the Henry family who retained it for more than 30 years and it has since changed hands several times. Captain Michael Henry still lives nearby in a house converted from the old estate laundry.

A TV film loosely based on Forman's book entitled *My Life So Far* and starring Colin Firth, Malcolm McDowell, Rosemary Harris and Mary Elizabeth Mastrantonio, was made in 1999. But for the purposes of the story the family home was moved from Beattock to Kiloran in the Highlands.

> One of the more unusual activities carried on at **Craigielands** during War War 1 was the processing of sphagnum moss for despatch to the front for field dressings.
>
> At that time it was virtually impossible to obtain cotton from the usual foreign sources and the moss, highly absorbent and mildly antiseptic, was a useful substitute.
>
> The operation, part of a national war effort, was organised by **Adam Forman** with the help of the Women's Auxiliary Corps and even local schoolchildren were recruited to help. Lorries from various parts of the country arrived at the estate with the dripping sackfuls which were emptied and spread on frames on the tennis courts to dry. Then after a number of simple processes, carried out on machines invented by Forman, it was shredded, packed and sent off. For his efforts, Forman was awarded the CBE.
>
> His son Denis, in his autobiography Son of Adam, recalls "all manner of sphagnum detritus" being piled into the Moss Room. "There were wooden mono-rails and wide flat sleepers and two-wheeled wooden trolley-like giant scooters," he adds. "There were jute sacks in their thousands, frames, Heath Robinson machines of all kinds ... and in one corner, like grain in a Pharaoh's tomb, a dusty pile of sphagnum moss itself."
>
> He said his father's close association with sphagnum moss during the war years left him with an exaggerated notion of its merits.
>
> "He claimed it to be both antiseptic and therapeutic and he caused to be manufactured, God knows where and how, not only sphagnum moss shaving soap but sphagnum moss toilet soap and sphagnum moss ointment," he recalled
>
> The Craigielands sphagnum moss venture is featured in the feature film *My Life So Far* starring Colin Firth as Adam Forman.

Focus on Farming

Agriculture has been the life-blood of the Beattock area since earliest times, dominating the culture of the people and providing the basis of the economy. Eking a living from the land has never been easy, however. The parish is in the Southern Uplands that form part of the Silurian belt, running from the Mull of Galloway to St Abb's Head in Berwickshire, and dating back more than 400 million years. The Silurian rocks are hard and massive, mainly whinstone, useful for road building but unsuitable for farming. The soil is fairly shallow, making cultivation difficult, although a stretch of land running along the bank of the Annan, about two miles wide and eight miles long, is more fertile than the rest of the parish.

Archaeologists have established that at the beginning of the first millennium AD, there was wholesale clearance of forests in this part of south-west Scotland, leaving open landscape where Iron Age tribes grew crops and reared animals in unenclosed ridged fields and rough pasture.

This system of communal farming, inefficient in land use, continued for hundreds of years until improvements brought a transformation during the agrarian revolution towards the end of the 18th century. The countryside underwent dramatic and sudden changes: land was enclosed with fences, stone dykes or thorn hedges, crop rotations were introduced and farms began to take on the shape that still exists to this day.

The reports on Kirkpatrick Juxta in the *Old* and *New Statistical Accounts* chart the progress. Writing in 1790, the parish minister Rev Gabriel Scott indicated that much of the land was still unenclosed in his time. He wrote: "The condition of the people might, in my humble opinion, be much ameliorated if the proprietors of land would grant them longer leases and better houses and either enclose their grounds or encourage their tenants to do so. By this means many acres not worth more than at present one shilling (5p) a year might be improved so as to yield 12s (60p) or 15s (75p)."

A rosier picture is painted 45 later by the Rev Dr William Singer, author of *A General View of Agriculture in the County of Dumfries*. In his 1834 article on the parish for the *New Statistical Account* he reported that farm buildings and fences were "in a constant state of progressive improvement". Land under the plough had been enhanced by draining, fencing and manuring and the production of green crops had raised the standard of livestock. He advocated further investment to turn more barren moorland into cultivated fields and moss into meadow.

Dr Singer's book includes a note by John Murray, of Murraythwaite, near Ecclefechan, who reported that the improvement and cultivation of Annandale had made rapid advances. "Consequently the appearance of every part of it has been almost incredibly altered for the better," he wrote.

Beattock

"Although rents have risen in a very great degree, the farmers, labourers and other inhabitants are now more wealthy, live better and are better fed and clothed than they were formerly."

The accuracy of the figures for land use and livestock recorded by the parish writers has been questioned but they provide the most reliable agricultural statistics available. Along with the official parish statistics gathered since 1866 they help to show the main trends in farming over the last two centuries - generally a move away from crop production to livestock management. As the road system improved it was often cheaper to buy grain than to produce it.

At the time Dr Singer wrote, there were 42 farms in the parish with 220 agricultural labourers, 46 female servants and 12 male servants. Around 7,000 acres (more than one-third of the parish's total farmland) was under the plough compared with just 438 acres at the end of the 18th century. The herds of Galloway cattle and flocks of Cheviot and black-faced sheep had also been greatly improved. Land rents had increased to £1 an acre for arable land and 5s (25p) for good hill pastures. The lowest farm rents were £150 with only three above £600 and one above £2,000.

Singer estimated the total rent of the parish as around £5,000. By his time, leases for arable land were granted for 15 to 21 years while sheep farms were leased for 13 years.

During the next century the amount of land under tillage dropped considerably - from 1,173 acres in 1866 to 933 in 1955 when oats and turnips were the main crops. The rest of the farmland was used as rough grazings. Over the same period, livestock increased dramatically. The number of cattle doubled to a total of 2,169 and sheep increased by over 40 per cent to 17,244.

In 1851 at the time of the first census, there were 35 farmers in the parish, employing about 120 labourers. The farmers' families would also work on the land. There were also associated trades such as blacksmiths, five of whom are listed.

Between 1851 and 1876, Beattock Inn took on an agricultural role - as venue for the important annual sheep sales. Up to 1,000 rams of different breeds went under the hammer at each auction, held annually on the day before the Moffat Fair.

Writer Henry Hall Dixon, of Carlisle, whose nom-de-plume was The Druid, provided a description of a sale in 1860, quoted by John A. Thomson in *Ring of Memories*, his book about Scottish auction marts.

It states: "The old inn hard by the bridge which spans the Evan Water looked quite bright that day with tables spread in the coach-houses and union jacks floating from the hay-loft. As visitors dropped in, table after table was added till the last coach house threw out the skirmishers with knife and fork half way across the yard.

"There was no music save the drone of the bagpipe in the distance and no blackface on the field save a negro who sold sweetmeats and treated each

Cheviot-breeding sahib to a most reverend salaam. Fully 100 shepherd dogs lay about or under the platforms and around the plaided crowd there walked an Edinburgh horse dealer with his hands in his pockets and trying hard to appreciate that cock of the lug and glint of the eye for which the Moodlaw flock is so famed. All the tups had been collected two or three days before at Mr Brydon's farm, Kinnelhead, and therefore most of the breeders know them by hearts."

Bertram Smith, an author and farmer, gives a good description of the sheep farms in Crashie Howe, his thinly disguised portrait of Kirkpatrick Juxta written in the 1920s. Sheep farming, he wrote, is "redeemed from monopoly by the grand scale on which it is practised and gains dignity from its exalted neighbourhood of crag and hill and heather". He added: "The land is not parcelled out or measured or enclosed - often the march between one farm and another is no more than an unseen line across the moor, well known to the wise sheep on either hand".

Although the parish remained mainly agricultural, many changes had taken place in the previous 120 years, as Sheila G. Forman reported in the *Third Statistical Account* in the 1950s. Due to the government policy during World War 2, the establishment of the Marketing Board and the high price of milk, dairying had replaced sheep farming to a great extent. (Although she does not mention it, the import of cheap beef from the Argentine was also a factor). Of the 14 dairy farms, some had herds of more than 50 cows, mainly Ayrshires. The parish still had a few sheep farms and several marginal farms.

Between 1939 and 1958, 61 acres of woodland and scrubland were felled and cleared. The Forestry Commission bought much of Auchen Castle estate and by 1974 it also owned parts of Craigielands estate.

During World War 2, Miss Forman explained, the Agricultural Executive Committee had insisted on a good deal of ploughing of old pastures and proper manuring to the great improvement of most of the farms. "The parish farmers were most co-operative and there were no cases of bad farming or dispossession," she wrote.

One major change occurred in 1965 when the trustees of the late Evelyn Wentworth Hope-Johnstone, who had died the previous year, put a large chunk of Annandale Estates under the hammer to pay death duties.

The 23,000 acres that were sold included several farms and other properties in Kirkpatrick Juxta. A further eight farms in the parish were sold in 1968 to the Crown Commissioners who already owned property in Annandale. Kinnelhead, one of the properties disposed of in 1965, was the area's largest sheep farm extending to 7424 acres of hill terrain.

Its rental at that time was £1019 19s 3d. Eighty-five years earlier, in 1880, the value was almost double (due to the First Boer War when wool was in big demand for military uniforms). The rent dropped to £1500 in 1924 and to a

Beattock

mere £500 in 1932 during the Great Depression. The figures are an interesting economic barometer.

Radical Changes

As elsewhere in Scotland, agriculture in Kirkpatrick Juxta had changed radically by the beginning of the 21st century. Farms had amalgamated to make them more economical or had been taken over by the Forestry Commission. Extensive mechanisation had led to a massive reduction in the number of workers while the introduction of television and other modern entertainment and pastimes had contributed to the demise of country pursuits like agricultural shows and sheepdog trials, once the highlighhts of the farming year.

George Paterson, who farms 550 acres at Dyke and Lochhouse but lives in Moffat, reflects the changes.

He said: "I'm predominantly a sheep farmer, producing about 1,000 lambs a year. In my father's time, lambs sold at £30 a head at Lockerbie market. Today they fetch £45 - an increase of only 50%. In my father's day £1 bought 4 gallons of petrol or eight pints of lager. What does it buy today? I would need to sell lambs at £600 a head to have an income equivalent to my father's.

"Last year I made £20,000 from the sale of lambs and the Single Farm Payment. But my feed bill was £18,000 and I had other expenses such as vet's bills on top of that. I reckon only two farms out of 10 make a profit today and it's not going to get any better."

George's family has played a major role in farming in Kirkpatrick Juxta for over a century. At various times his grandfather and father farmed at Holms, Tathhill and Buckrigg which was originally run by George's great-uncle, the late William Paterson, principal of the West of Scotland Agricultural College until his retirement in 1944.

George added: "After World War 2 we were told by the government to produce as much food as possible. Nowadays, they are not bothered about stock as long as the farm looks good.

"There have been lots of other changes. My father, who farmed until he died at the age of 80, used to travel to Oban to buy hill lambs. They were sent down by train to Beattock. He then walked them two miles to the farm. He also used to walk stock from Buckrigg to Holms - two miles down the dual carriageway on a Sunday morning."

Craigielands Hill Farm overlooks Beattock, and is run by John Quigley, a third generation Beattock farmer, and his son James. He tells much the same story.

John's father Tom moved to the area as a single ploughman - probably from Torthorwald - at the end of the 19th century and worked first at Newbank Farm,

Focus on Farming

about four miles south of Beattock. He got married in the parish and later took a new job at Craigielands estate. When the grieve retired, he was given the post and in the 1930s rented Craigielands Hill. It is now owned by the Quigleys.

"In my father's time there were seven or eight men on the farm and at busy times estate workers would also be called in to lend a hand," said John. "Now there are just two of us and my son's wife who does the paperwork. But we're still using pretty old-fashioned methods - just growing enough to feed the animals."

The 356-acre farm, 650 feet above sea level, has 280 breeding ewes, 60 Texel-cross ewes and 55 cows whose calves are sold as store cattle.

John, who joined his father on the farm after leaving the local school at 15, insists that making a living is not easy. "Without government subsidies and the 'less favoured area' grant we wouldn't be here," he said. "Everyone tells us we have a wonderful view . . .but we can't live on the view.'

Another prominent farming family are the Smiths. Their link with the area goes back to the early part of last century when Alex (Sandy) Smith, born at Tinto, Lanarkshire, took the tenancy of Beattock Farm in the middle of the village. The farm was part of the estate of Beattock House, owned by grocery tycoon Thomas Bishop.

Grandpa Smith, as he is still called by the family, had six sons and two daughters.

His grandson Robert, also a farmer and the inspiration for this book, recalled: "My grandfather believed in living a simple life. Once when he was presented with a tea service on some special occasion, he said it was too grand and insisted it be taken back.

"His business was buying lambs for slaughter. He opened an abattoir at Beattock Farm where carcasses were prepared for Smithfield Market in London. They were loaded in a railway siding beside the farm."

Robert Smith has a repertoire of stories illustrating how farming has changed.

"Until 1947", he said, "farmers' tax was based on the rent they paid their landlord but in that year the government decided they would be dealt with like any other business, and they were sent forms by the Inland Revenue.

"One local farmer wasn't impressed. He wrote back: 'Dear Inspector, Thank you for the form but I'm sending it back as I don't want to join the scheme meantime'. It shows what a difference 60 years can make."

The day-to-day running of the farm was also very different a few generations ago. Robert recalls how his father used to walk sheep from Lanarkshire to Beattock, stopping half-way overnight and then carrying on down the A74.

Most of Sandy Smith's descendants have kept up the farming tradition. Robert's cousin, Margaret Moffat, born in 1931 and still living in Beattock, proved at an early age that women can play an important role on the land.

Beattock

FARMER John Quigley still uses old-style methods down on the farm.

Focus on Farming

ROBERT SMITH, a third generation Beattock man of farming stock, has a repertoire of stories about the area.

The daughter of agricultural contractor and champion ploughman, Thomas Marshall, she remembers driving a tractor when she was just 13.

"I started on a wee orange Fordson and then a Fordson Major," she recalled. "My feet couldn't reach the pedals and I had to drive standing up. I really enjoyed it."

The biggest sheep farm in Kirkpatrick Juxta in these days was Kinnelhead. At its busiest, it took six shepherds to look after the hirsel. One of them was Walter Brydon who worked there from 1947 till he retired in 1960.

His daughter Helen Wright, of Beattock, has memories of what life was like on the hill farm. "We had 10 score of Cheviots and 20 score of Blackfaces," she said. "It was always busy with the lambing, clipping, dipping and marketing. There was also the peat to be cut and put out to dry.

"As a teenager I used to help with the lambing and clipping. Going to the markets in Lockerbie and Lanark was the highlight. The shepherds preferred Lanark. . .they said they got better prices there."

She added: "We were never lonely at Kinnelhead, there were so many shepherds and their families. We had barn dances once or twice a year. A band came from Wamphray and the herds' wives provided the food. The rural meetings in the village hall were very popular with the women. We caught up with all the gossip."

Retired farmer Graham Gardiner, who tenanted Biggarts Farm in Kirkpatrick Juxta till 1992, recalled that at the beginning of the war he was compelled to produce 40 acres of corn, double the quantity he grew previously.

At that time he was still ploughing with horses on the 250-acre mixed farm that had about 150 dairy and beef cattle and the same number of sheep.

Seeds were sown broadcast and crops were stalked in the old-fashioned way. "The corn was cut and put in stooks and left for a fortnight, then built into stacks," he said. "There was an art in stacking. If the stacks were properly built, you didn't need to thatch them to keep them dry."

The threshing machine, drawn by a traction engine, came to the farm twice a year and neighbouring farmers would roll up their sleeves and help with the work. This reciprocal arrangement known as "neighbouring" also operated at the sheep clipping, all done with hand shears.

Beattock

In the years immediately after World War 2, there was no mains electricity at Biggarts. Power was supplied by "a wee Lister engine" and the main lights were Tilly lamps. The farm had no bulk milk tank and the daily yield had to be taken in 10-gallon tanks to Beattock Station.

But times were changing. The post-war years saw the impact of mechanisation that was to revolutionise agriculture. Graham got his first tractor, a Ferguson TE-20 - the famous Wee Grey Fergie - in 1946 and his first diesel in 1954. The following year, he obtained his first baler - "the best thing since sliced bread".

Mains electricity first came to the farm in 1951 but it was the 1970s before a bulk milk tank was installed. "Life gradually got easier" said Graham.

Famous Folk

A leading Scottish statesman who helped frame our history, a TV boss who gave us some of our most popular programmes, a football international, a writer of ripping yarns and a family who produced a best-selling brew... these are just some of the famous folk from Kirkpatrick Juxta. Their stories are all part of the parish's colourful story.

Religious Fighter

Kirkpatrick Juxta's most famous son is Archibald Johnston, Lord Warriston (1611-63) - advocate, statesman, judge, member of the Scottish and English Parliaments and of the House of Lords and father of 13. Described by writer Thomas Carlyle as "a lynx-eyed lawyer and austere Presbyterian zealot, full of fire, of heavy energy and gloom", he was a key political player in one of the most turbulent periods of British history.

As a leader in the fierce struggle to maintain the Presbyterian religion, he helped to draft the Articles of the National Covenant, the 1638 manifesto to consolidate opposition to Charles I's attempts to impose Anglicanism on the Presbyterian Church. It was this document, described as the most important in the history of Scotland, that gave the Covenanters their name.

Lord Warriston

Archibald, son of James Johnston, a minor landowner in Kirkpatrick Juxta parish and a merchant burgess in Edinburgh, is said to have been born in 1611 at Beirholm ("Barley Lands") a farmhouse on what is now Milton Farm and no longer in existence. The exact date of his birth is unknown but it is recorded that he was baptised on March 28, 1611. From his early years, he was religious to the point of being neurotic. His diary relates how he "roared, youled (howled) and pitifully skirled (screamed)" in his devotional torments and it has been said by one eminent historian that he was no mere religious fanatic but "a man walking on the dizzy verge of madness". As a young man, he apparently had no objection to the episcopal establishment but Charles' attempts to force the new English-style service book on the kirk threw him to the side of the opposition and he became completely obsessed with the concept of a perpetual contract between the people of Scotland and Scotland's God.

Johnston studied law at Glasgow University and was admitted as an advocate at the Scottish bar in Edinburgh at the age of 22. Five years later, he was appointed one of the five advocates to advise the Presbyterian Commission of the Tables, a curiously named committee formed to resist Charles' impositions. This was Johnston's stepping stone to the very centre of the religious and political maelstrom of the era.

Johnston devised a plan to counter each royal proclamation with the reading of a "protestation" which was registered with legal formalities. But his greatest achievement was conceiving and co-writing the National Covenant which brought to a head the growing campaign against the royal religious innovations. It demanded a free Scottish parliament and free general assembly with no interference by the king whose task, it declared, was to maintain the purity of the kirk.

On the last day of February, 1638, Johnston read the document to the leading Scottish nobles and presbyters assembled at Greyfriars kirkyard in Edinburgh. It was then laid on a flat rock or tombstone for them to sign and about 150 affixed their names. Johnston described the signing in his diary as "that glorious marriage day of the kingdom with God". The following day clergy and burgesses followed suit and the Covenant was then distributed to the four corners of Scotland to be subscribed by all. Some are said to have signed in their own blood.

Presbyterianism was fundamentally incompatible with Charles I's belief in the divine right of kings and confrontation was inevitable. In the countdown to hostilities Johnston, now clerk to the Tables and to the General Assembly, was a leading player.

At the General Assembly at Glasgow in 1638, his ability to produce ancient registers condemning episcopacy had a considerable bearing on the kirk's decision to depose bishops.

This was a major factor in the complete breakdown of relations between Charles and his Scottish subjects. The king decided on a show of force and advanced with a rabble army towards the Border but in the so-called Bishop's War his forces were no match for the Covenanters, strengthened by veteran soldiers from the Thirty Years War in Europe. Their general Alexander Leslie occupied the north of England and Charles quickly sought a truce. Johnston took part in the negotiations leading to the Pacification of Berwick in 1639 that brought the military conflict to an end for the time being.

The king agreed to attend both Parliament and the general assembly in an attempt to appease the Covenanters. On his arrival in Scotland in 1641, Johnston led the opposition on the important constitutional point of the control of state appointments. He received public thanks from the Scottish Parliament and as a token of the king's policy of conciliation was knighted and appointed a Lord of Session (a judge) with the title of Lord Warriston - a name derived from an estate he had purchased near Edinburgh. In the same month he was appointed

Famous Folk

to represent Scotland in a commission at Westminster to settle the affairs of Scotland and was largely responsible for drawing up the so-called Treaty of Uxbridge which, however, failed to resolve the differences between the two countries. The last chance of ending the war by compromise had gone.

Besides his public duties in England, Johnston represented the county of Edinburgh in the Scottish Parliament from 1643 to 1647 and was speaker of the barons. After the final defeat of Charles in October 1646, he was made King's Advocate (the chief law officer of the Crown, later known as Lord Advocate) and voted £3,000 by Parliament for his services.

Two years later, the king's party in the Scottish parliament triumphed and formed a famous "engagement" to support Charles, then a prisoner at Carisbrook Castle on the Isle of Wight. The deal was: the King would establish Presbyterianism in Scotland and in England for three years in exchange for a Scottish army to enforce the terms of the pact. Johnston was furious and became leader of the Remonstrants, the extreme Covenanters who opposed the Engagement.

After the defeat of the Engagers by Cromwell's New Model Army at Preston in 1648, Johnston was initially opposed to the Lord Protector's regime but latterly came to terms with it and took his seat in a new parliament as Commissioner for Argyllshire. But their relationship was interrupted by the execution of Charles I and the proclamation of Charles II as King in Edinburgh in February 1649 on condition he accepted the Covenant.

The following month Johnston was appointed Lord Clerk Register (responsible for the Scottish archives). He still held political power and in 1650 he passed sentence of death on James Graham, 5th Earl of Montrose, the brilliant former Covenanter who commanded the royalist side in Scotland during the civil war, and ordered him to be hanged, drawn and quartered.

In the years that followed, however, Johnston lost his offices and seems to have been reduced to poverty but in 1656 he was one of the representatives of the Remonstrants who went to London to make their peace with Cromwell. The Lord Protector confirmed him in his position as Lord Clerk Register and appointed him a commissioner for the administration of justice in Scotland. He was included in Cromwell's new House of Lords.

Johnston's days as a leading statesmen, however, were numbered. At the restoration of Charles II in 1660, he was singled out for punishment and had a sum of 100 pounds Scots on his head. He avoided capture and escaped to Holland and then to Germany. He was condemned to death in his absence in 1661 for high treason. Two years later, having ventured into France to meet his wife, he was captured at Rouen and with the consent of King Louis XIV was sent to England for trial. He was convicted of accepting office under Cromwell after being King's Advocate and was publicly executed in 1663 at the Mercat Cross in Edinburgh. His body was beheaded and his head displayed on the Netherbow Port of the city. Johnston was buried in Greyfriars Churchyard in

Edinburgh where 25 years earlier he had read the National Covenant to the Scottish nobles. In his will he left 100 merks Scots to the parish church of Kirkpatrick Juxta.

Beattock's Braveheart

The 1st Earl of Moray's daughter Black Agnes, who was born and brought up at Auchencass in Kirkpatrick Juxta, went on to become one of Scotland's greatest heroines... a medieval Amazon and female Braveheart.

Married to the 9th Earl of Dunbar and March, she was left in charge of the family castle at Dunbar while her husband was away on duty with King David II. In 1337, an English force led by William Montague, Earl of Salisbury, besieged the stronghold. He may have anticipated an easy victory but failed to take into account the courage and determination of Black Agnes, so named because of her dusky complexion and raven hair.

Acting as a bold and valiant commander, she repelled all the English attacks that lasted for five months. Salisbury began by catapulting huge rocks at the castle walls. The doughty Agnes cocked a snook at him by sending her maids dressed in their finest on to the ramparts to remove the marks left by the missiles with clean white handkerchiefs. Salisbury opened his second phase by rolling a huge battering ram at the gate. Agnes countered by signalling for a massive boulder to be dropped, smashing the ram, killing some of the besiegers and scattering others.

The cunning Salisbury then bribed a gatekeeper to leave the gate unlocked. He accepted the money but promptly informed Agnes of the ploy. As a small party slipped into the fortress the portcullis was swiftly lowered and Salisbury's trusty squire was taken prisoner. In desperation, the earl then tried to starve the castle into submission by cutting off all contact with the outside world.

Just as supplies ran out, help arrived in the person of Sir Alexander Ramsay of Dalhousie with 40 men in two boats. They entered the castle through a half-submerged tunnel and next morning made a surprise attack on the English, slaying many and taking prisoners. On June 10, 150 days after the siege began, Salisbury finally admitted defeat.

Black Agnes remains a Scottish icon celebrated in ballads and poems:

> *"And do they come?" Black Agnes cried,*
> *Nor storm, nor midnight stops our foes;*
> *Well, then, the battle's chance be tried,*
> *The Thistle shall out-thorn the Rose.*

Famous Folk

She spake, and started from her bed,
And cased her lovely limbs in mail;
The helmet on her coal-black head,
Sluiced o'er her eyes - an iron veil!

In her fair hand she grasped a spear,
A baldrick o'er her shoulders flung,
While loud the bugle-note of war,
From Dunbar's cavern'd echoes rung.

Salisbury himself or some of his followers are said to have composed a verse at the end of the siege:

She kept a stir in tower and trench,
That brawling, boisterous Scottish wench:
Came I early, came I late,
I found Agnes at the gate.

Sir Walter Scott wrote of her: "From the record of Scottish heroes, none can pressure to erase her." Certainly, she is Kirkpatrick Juxta's most celebrated daughter.

Fitba' Frolics

Beattock can boast an international footballer among its distinguished sons. True, Jamie Niven, who played for Moffat FC and Glasgow Rangers in the late 19th century, was capped only once for Scotland but he was an outstanding player of his time and even wrote a book about Scottish football.

He reached the peak of his career on Saturday, March 14, 1885, when he was a defender in the Scotland team that defeated Ireland 8-2 before a 6,000-strong crowd in the original Hampden Park in Glasgow.

Jamie Niven

Niven, the son of a farmer at Longbedholm, about five miles north of Beattock, was born in 1861. Apparently he did not follow in his father's footsteps and in the 1881 census is described as a grocer.

As a lad, he played for Evanwater Shepherds. He recalls in his book that one game against the Caley navvies (the builders of the Caledonian Railway) lasted about three hours and was watched by a big crowd. But the challenge was never repeated.

MOFFAT FC, the team for which Niven played before joining Glasgow Rangers.

Association football with proper rules was introduced into the area by the Rev W.H. Churchill, the co-founder of St Ninian's School in Moffat with A.J.C. Dowding (father of Air Chief Marshal Dowding of Battle of Britain fame),

During his short stay in the town, Rev Churchill, who had been an all-round sportsman at Cambridge University, founded Moffat FC and donated a trophy - the first to be competed for in the South of Scotland. Soon fitba' fever raged throughout the district and, as the team became established and its support grew, locals even wrote poems about it.

In the early days the boys played in brass-toed clogs and one wore his sister's old high-heeled boots. Eventually, the team got its strip - narrow black and white stripes like Queens Park - but there seems to have been no strict dress code.

Niven tells the story of how his fellow player Alex Robertson on one occasion swopped his ankle-length white trousers for skin-tight pants in the team colours greatly to the amusement of the crowd who quickly nick-named him The Zebra. All went well till the second half when he clashed with an opponent and ripped his pants. "The crowd laughed and so did the players," wrote Niven. "A friend came to the rescue with an overcoat to escort Alex off the ground."

Full-back David Brown could not play without his bonnet. If it was knocked off, it did not matter whether the goal was in jeopardy or not, he ignored the

> One of Scotland's pioneer photographers, **John Rutherford**, was born at New Farm, south of Beattock village in 1842. At the age of 15, he left for Bristol where he set up as a draper and prospered. He sold his business in 1875 and bought Jardington estate near Newbridge, Dumfries. A man of many talents, he was a woodcarver and clockmaker as well as a photographer. He contributed scientific papers to Dumfries and Galloway Antiquarian Society and is credited with having installed the first telephone in Galloway. He died in 1925, aged 82.

ball and dashed across the pitch to retrieve his precious bunnet.

The match officials were no less eccentric. Dr Scott, one of the team's best supporters, occasionally acted as a touch-line steward (linesman). Armed with a staff, he prevented the crowd from invading the pitch. In a cup-tie against the 5th KRV (Kirkcudbrightshire Rifle Volunteers) one of the players hit the doctor's tall hat with the ball, sending it flying into the crowd.

"Without waiting for the recovery of his headgear, he chased the supposed culprit - who was not the real offender - all over the field with his staff in a striking position amidst roars of laughter from the crowd," recalled Niven. "But the incident did not prevent him taking up his position at the next match."

Some of the matches were hilarious. When Niven's team met Burnside Rovers from Partick at Moffat on New Year's Day 1882, it was obvious many of the visiting side had been first-footing and were still under the weather. The goalkeeper was in such a state, he was asked to stand down but insisted he was in charge of the goalposts. In fact, he was afraid to let go of them. Each time he did so in his attempt to catch the ball he fell flat on his face amidst roars of laughter from the spectators. He was substituted in the second half but the home team still had a resounding 9-1 victory. The antics of the Glasgow XI no doubt caused some tut-tutting among the unco guid who, says Niven, "used to shake their heads and denounce us for playing on fast days." (The twice-yearly fast days were still widely observed at that time, especially in country districts and are often referred to in the Beattock school log.)

The huge wages paid to today's footballers would have shocked the Moffat men of these times. All they received for their efforts was a meal after the match if they were lucky. Sometimes, the reward was no more than a jug of brown ale, bread and cheese.

Beattock

Niven travelled with the Moffat club as far north as the Central Belt and south to Liverpool. Their keenest fought matches were the ties for the coveted Churchill Cup. The fierce rivalry between local teams is illustrated by the story of how one Moffat player had to be kept under wraps - literally to ensure he could turn out for a vital semi-final.

Niven discovered ace half-back William Edgar, who occasionally also turned out for Glasgow Northern, had promised to play for them in their English Christmas tour. If this had been confirmed he would have been excluded from the cup and, sure enough, a deputation from Moffat's opponents were at Dumfries station to look out for him on the midnight mail train as it travelled south with the Northern team.

They went to the carriage window and told the team a friend from Moffat was looking for Edgar - a ruse to get him to show himself. But it did not work. His team-mates, who were party to the deception, "were using the crack half-back as a foot-warmer covered with a rug." When the train pulled out of the station they unveiled him amidst loud cheers. Niven concludes that since Edgar was Moffat-born and learned his football in Annandale, the local side was fully justified in playing him despite his appearance with the Glasgow team.

Another cup-tie was put at risk when a key Moffat player was charged with malicious mischief - lifting gates off their hinges! He was due to appear in the burgh court on the Saturday of the match at high noon . . . 10 minutes before the train was due to leave. Niven had a word in advance with the provost - a team patron - who was to sit on the bench and he obligingly brought the case to the top of the court list and promptly fined the offending footballer five shillings (25p) with the alternative of seven days in jail. The player was broke but Niven produced the fine and they dashed off to the station just in time to catch the train. They played a great game and won the tie.

Sadly, interest in the Churchill Cup declined over the years and it was eventually returned to its donor who kept it for a while but eventually began to hate the sight of it. He had the names erased by a silversmith and traded it in.

Niven's book faithfully recounts details of Moffat FC's notable matches, kick by kick in some cases, and recalls many of the players. Disappointingly, he has very little to say about himself, apart from revealing that he had an offer from Notts County (which he declined), that he played for a season with Glasgow Rangers and that his 1885 international was his "principal honour".

Mouth music appears in almost every culture in one form or another. In the Beattock area it was known as **deedling** - a word also used to describe the handing down of pipe tunes orally.

Author Bertram Smith describes "deedling" in his 1921 book *Crashie Howe*, a thinly disguised picture of Beattock.

"The deedle, not singing and clearly not humming, is perhaps the most primitive form of emitting rhythmical sound," he explains. "By the simple and continuous rise of the tongue against the roof of the mouth, the notes are given out to unchanging syllables repeated indefinitely - deedle, deedle, deedle, dee.

"With his whole soul he plies his art, throwing in all his resources as he calls forth rhythm from the motion of his head, a fainting expression from his bobbing knees, emphasis from his swaying arms."

The custom, according to Smith, died out in the 1840s.

Ripping Yarns

Beattock's best known literary figure, talented author and journalist Bertram Smith, was not born in the area but spent most of his life there and was a native by adoption.

The son of James Smith, a cotton broker in Liverpool, he was born in nearby New Brighton, Cheshire, in 1876. His connection with Beattock began when his father bought Craigielands mansion in 1882. Bertram, his four brothers - one of whom became headmaster of Loretto School in Edinburgh - and his sister all spent their early years there.

Bertram Smith

After leaving school - the boys were all educated at Loretto - Bertram joined the family cotton firm on Merseyside but still returned to Beattock whenever he could. He was dogged throughout his life with TB and decided from an early age to give up city life and settle in the country for the good of his health.

He bought Broomlands Farm in Beattock where he successfully combined agriculture with writing. He produced seven books and contributed to the Manchester Guardian, Country Life, Punch and his local paper, the Annandale Herald, under the pen-name Bis. He was special correspondent for the Scotsman

Beattock

at curling bonspiels in Kandersteg in the Bernese Oberland - an assignment combining his loves of sport and writing. He also wrote several plays and comedy sketches and appeared in some of them in Beattock Village Hall.

Bertram probably inherited his literary talents from his mother Amy who wrote two novels *Vida* and *Claire* and tried her hand at poetry. While her books (long since forgotten) were typical Victorian stories about the fortunes of young girls in the throes of growing up, Bertram's were mostly ripping schoolboy yarns and tales of the outdoor life.

He had a rare gift for remembering the minutest details of his boyhood exploits and the ability to write about them in a crisp and racy style with a touch of whimsical humour. He had an extraordinary gift for fun, a quiet unexpected dry champagne sort of bubbling up of verbal high spiritedness, wrote one reviewer.

Many of his stories are based on his exploits at Craigielands where as a young man he teamed up with two of his brothers, his brother-in-law and a friend to form the Palship, a group devoted to comradeship and sporting prowess.

His nephew Sir Denis Forman in his autobiography *Son of Adam* describes the activities of this close-knit brotherhood formed originally to navigate local rivers in homemade punts. The group successfully made trips down the Annan, Nith, Esk and Tweed with Bertram (nicknamed BS) as the Grand Punt Master. The Pals also took part in a range of other activities including shooting, swimming, tenting, walking and winter sports as well as amateur theatricals.

Another of Bertram's abiding interests was caravanning. He began with a horse-drawn covered wagon and later designed his own caravans, owning at one time a fleet of eight. They were built by virtuoso local carpenter Johnnie Thomson whose other notable achievements were a prize-winning model caravan and a wooden house for World War 1 Belgian refugees.

Bertram's many trips, including a marathon from the Border to John o' Groats, provided material for his first book, *The Whole Art of Caravanning*, published in 1907, and another, *Caravanning Days*, seven years later. In the years between, he wrote *Totty: a Tale of Ten Exciting Terms*, a school story for the boys' *Commander* annual in 1908. Almost a century later, *Totty* is still being read by aficionados of boys' yarns on the Internet. It was serialised in Paul Edmund Norman's online magazine *Gateway* between December 2004 and June 2005.

Bertram's two other school stories, *A Perfect Genius*, published in 1909, and *Running Wild*, which appeared in 1920 after his death, are riotous boyhood romps, written by one who always remained a boy, according to a contemporary. A series of essays that he entitled *Days of Discovery*, published in 1917, also illustrates his remarkable recollections of childhood, even his days in the nursery.

Famous Folk

Of special interest to Beattock is Bertram's book *Crashie Howe a Hill Parish*, a thinly disguised study of Kirkpatrick Juxta, its scenery and wealth of characters.

The fictional Crashie Howe with its one church, one school, one shop and one road is "attractive to curlers and all directly or sympathetically interested in sheep" and is ruled by the shop at the bridge or rather by Aggie the shopkeeper. She has succeeded her mother and made the shop a powerful instrument of government.

He adds: "We of the upper parish enjoy all the special benefits of living out of sight at the end of a road that leads to nowhere. Thus it comes about that our life is entirely free from any burden of perplexity."

Crashie Howe, like Beattock, has its parish council, school board, registrar and inspector of poor, all regarded with good humoured tolerance "for we know we are in no need of constituted authority. We are well content to be ruled by the shop".

When the book appeared it was hailed as "a well deserved appreciation of the great patient and silent courage with which Scottish peasants meet the ills of life" though one critic observed that Smith did not find much beauty or softness in the Scottish character.

Bertram, tall and broad-shouldered, was himself a tough and courageous character who put up a gallant fight against his illness and never let it deter his love for the rain and the hills or his enthusiasm for sport. He was an active farmer with new ideas - he helped popularise ploughing by tractor to increase the acreage under crop during World War 1 and started a potato club to encourage locals to dig for victory. He also helped organise the collection and preparation of sphagnum moss, used for dressing wounds on the battlefield.

Soon after the war started, Bertram helped find accommodation and work for some of the Belgian refugees who arrived in Britain after their country was overrun by the Germans in 1914. In an article in Punch he launched a Sporpot (savings box) scheme to raise money to aid their return home after four and a half years in exile. He also donated an ambulance and two caravans for use by Belgian soldiers at the front.

Despite his illness Bertram led an active and varied life and immersed himself in village life. He had a reputation as a benefactor of the poor and as a kindly, good-natured country gentleman who was popular with everyone.

'In spite of the burdens he bore, he remained a boy with a boy's ideals, a boy's high sense of honour and a boy's capacity for laughter," wrote an admirer of his work. He died in 1918 when he was just 41 and was buried in Kirkpatrick Juxta churchyard. His wife Freda survived him by 12 years.

Beattock

Beetle Mania

One of the most successful businessmen ever to make his home in Beattock was Thomas G. Bishop, a grocery tycoon with a passion for studying beetles.

He founded a chain of grocery stores that grew into a supermarket enterprise and then became Cooper FineFare. Cooper was the maiden name of an aunt who had lent him money to launch his own business after travelling in tea for Tetley's.

Thomas G. Bishop

Bishop, born in Carlisle in 1846, rented Beattock House in 1890 - about 20 years after it was built - and later purchased it. He became involved with the local community and was a Justice of the Peace for Dumfriesshire.

His interest in beetles took him all over Scotland to study and collect various species like the giant diving beetles on Eigg in the Outer Hebrides in 1911. He even had a species named after him.

Bishop also bought, mainly at auction, collections and rare specimens from famous 19th century naturalists including Charles Darwin, author of *On the Origin of Species*.

Bishop died in 1922 in Helensburgh where he also owned a house. His vast collection was left to Glasgow University's Hunterian Museum where it has proved invaluable for research and is still on display.

Bishop's family was uniquely linked in marriage with the family of Robert (Concrete Bob) McAlpine, founder of the building and civil engineering empire, who was created a baronet in 1918. Bishop's daughters Lillias and Margaret married Sir Robert's sons, Robert and William, and Bishop's son Andrew wed Sir Robert's daughter Mary. The three weddings (surely some sort of record) took place between 1892 and 1897.

William's eldest son, Thomas, who was educated at Warriston School in Moffat and became the fourth baronet in 1968, kept up his association with the area. His portrait hangs in Bankfoot House old people's home in Moffat which benefited from his generosity.

Miss Irene Park, of Moffat, who launched a fund in the 1960s to provide a residential home for the town, recalled how Sir Thomas donated £10,000, a sum that made possible the purchase of the house and the installation of central heating.

"He had a great love for the area dating back to his schooldays and his memories of Beattock House, the home of his maternal grandparents," she recalled. "When he died in 1983 his ashes were scattered on Beattock Hill." When Sir Thomas' brother and successor Robert, was made a life peer in 1979 he took the title Baron McAlpine of Moffat.

Agricultural Pioneer

William Paterson was a Beattock farmer who rose to the top in Scottish agriculture - as principal of the West of Scotland Agricultural College.

During his 33 years in the post, he made a valuable contribution to the knowledge of crop and animal husbandry and farm management and had a great influence on thousands of students.

He grew up with agricultural science, saw its early blossoming in the 1920s and 30s and throughout his career kept abreast of its rapid advance and its many expanding fringe subjects.

William Paterson

Paterson was born at Buckrigg Farm in 1878, the youngest of a family of 13. All seven sons and two of the six daughters took university degrees.

For six years before he began studying agricultural science he trained in the hard school of practice on the farm learning to plough, draw a drill, swing a scythe and build a stack. He graduated BSc (Agriculture) in 1905 and obtained the National Diploma in Agriculture with honours the same year.

His qualifications fitted him perfectly for an academic role and he became lecturer in agriculture in the Central College in Glasgow and later county lecturer and adviser in Dumfries.

He was appointed principal of the college and professor of agriculture in 1911 and for the following 33 years was responsible for the direction of the college in all its growing activities. When he retired in 1944, the University of Glasgow honoured him with an LLD degree.

During his long period in charge of the college, spanning two world wars, he saw many important developments in agricultural education and the application of science to farming. The Central College was twice extended and the dairy and poultry schools and the college farm were transferred from Kilmarnock to Auchencruive in Ayrshire. The college's sphere of influence in the counties also expanded, calling for more teaching and advisory staff.

Professor Paterson introduced a scheme of demonstration fields. An arrangement was made with a local farmer to put a field through a rotation of cropping, suggested by the college, as a means of showing the most modern proved methods of manuring and seeding. By this means much useful practical knowledge was disseminated at very little cost. Paterson took an intense interest in this work and was often present at the demonstrations.

At the college farms, he also carried out experiments on the nutrition of pigs and dairy cows, which revolutionised the industry.

Professor Paterson was admired by his colleagues not only as a leading agricultural scientist and administrator but also as a gifted teacher, lecturer and broadcaster.

Beattock

Away from work, he was a dedicated church member. For half a century he was organist and choirmaster at Hope Memorial Church in Wamphray and for 20 years he held a Sunday school in his own home for the children of Kirkpatrick Juxta.

Distinguished Brewers

Scotland's famous brewing dynasty, the Youngers, had close links with Kirkpatrick Juxta for more than a century and a half. Their family seats were two of the parish's most imposing houses - Craigielands and Auchen Castle - and succeeding generations became closely involved with the local community.

It was William Younger II (1767-1842) son of the founder of the Edinburgh brewing firm, who bought a 600-acre Beattock estate which he named Craigielands in 1805 for £7869 11s 9d. Twelve years later, he built the Palladian mansion of the same name.

At the time he moved into his Beattock home, he was already a prosperous businessman. But his life might well have gone in a different direction if it had not been for a loyal and rather ferocious dog!

As a boy he used to spend much of his time at La Mancha, the Peeblesshire home of Archibald Cochrane, 9th Earl of Dundonald, a friend of the family. While playing near the house, he was snatched by a gipsy who made off with

ONCE the home of the Youngers, Auchen Castle is now a luxury hotel.

him. But, according to the official story of the Youngers, "the lad was followed by a sagacious dog called Sancho who rushed to the attack with such vigour that the kidnapper took to his heels."

William studied at Edinburgh University in his teens and helped his mother run the family brewery in Leith. In 1793 he opened his own vaults for the sale of ale and porter and three years later set up his own brewhouse within the precincts of Holyrood Abbey. As the threat of a French invasion loomed in 1798, he joined the Edinburgh Volunteers along with Walter Scott and contributed to a fund to start soup kitchens in the city.

By 1802, William Younger II, described as a man of inherited vigour, vision and shrewd commercial instinct, was exporting Edinburgh ale to London where it was found 'to surpass the strength and flavour of any ever offered for sale'. He continued to expand his business and by the time he acquired the Beattock estate his brews had gained the highest reputation and his ale, beer and porter were on tap in inns and taverns throughout Scotland.

In 1821, with the deaths of his brother Archibald and his partner and brother-in-law Robert Hunter, William was able to consolidate the Younger interests and goodwill under a single roof. Four years after that he moved his brewery to the former townhouse of the Marquis of Lothian in the Canongate and soon expanded and extended into overseas markets.

William Younger II died in 1842 and was buried at Kirkpatrick Juxta kirkyard, leaving a highly successful business to his elder son William III (1801-54) who had originally trained for the Scottish bar. He saw the brewery develop its foreign trade and by the 1840s clippers were taking Edinburgh ale in large quantities to the other side of the world. He was in charge of the company when it marked it centenary in 1849. He was forced through ill health to give up active participation in the business and retired to Craigielands where he died in his early 50s and was also buried in the local churchyard.

The estate passed to William Younger IV (1831-86) who became the family's senior representative in the firm at the age of 23 and saw further expansions. He retained Craigielands for only three years before selling it to businessman William Colvin in 1857. It is said that on Colvin's death, the Youngers wanted to buy back Craigielands but they were apparently outbid by cotton broker James Smith, of Liverpool, who paid £50,000 for it in 1882.

In the meantime William IV had bought Auchen Castle estate in 1879 for £62,500. Its ornate house had been built in 1849 as the home farm for General Henry Butler-Johnstone who served with Sir Ralph Abercromby in Egypt during the Napoleonic Wars He was Conservative MP for Canterbury for two spells between 1852 and 1862 and was succeeded by his son who held the same seat until 1878. The estate included three cottages named after military campaigns - Egypt, Rosetta and Valenciennes - and, it is said, plantations were laid out to represent the disposition of British troops at the 1801 Battle of Abukir, ranked

Beattock

as one of the British Army's most daring and brilliant exploits.

The house had been altered and enlarged by the addition of two round turrets following a fire 20 years after it was built and it was a magnificent mansion when the Youngers moved in.

On William Younger IV's death in 1886, the estate passed to his only son - William V - who had no connection with the family brewing business. He joined the Army and later became a Unionist MP for a Lincolnshire seat, which he held from 1895 to 1906. A supporter of free trade, he opposed the Conservatives' tariff reform policy and switched to the Liberals, winning the Peebles and Selkirk seat for them in 1909.

Failing health prevented him from standing at the election the following year and he was made a baronet in the 1911 New Year Honours, taking the title Sir William Younger of Auchencastle. For the rest of his life he devoted himself to advocating better housing in Scotland which he believed would help prevent the spread of tuberculosis. He also worked for the repatriation of disabled servicemen and co-founded a London orthopaedic hospital. Until his death in 1937, he took a great interest in local activities. As chairman of the Beattock School board, he was a regular visitor to the classrooms. On one occasion in 1911, he "addressed the senior scholars on the necessity of teeth cleaning".

Sir William Younger

The school log added: "Through his generosity every child on the school roll is provided with a tooth brush and a tin of tooth powder to be used at school for a short period until there is reason to hope they may be regularly used at home." To mark the coronation of King George V the same year, Sir William and his wife planted oak trees in the playground and in 1913 they presented the pupils with photographs of themselves as a souvenir of their silver wedding.

Over the generations, the Youngers' ranks included distinguished businessmen, politicians and soldiers - even a VC. The first baronet's cousin Captain David Younger, aged 29, of 1 Bn Gordon Highlanders, won the supreme award for dragging an artillery wagon and a gun into shelter near Krugersdorp during the Boer War. He was wounded and died soon afterwards.

The Youngers added to the fame and distinction of Kirkpatrick Juxta but the family links with the parish were severed after World War 2. The second baronet, William Younger VI sold Auchencastle estate in 1946 though he retained the farm of Lawesknowe for a further eight years. The estate was bought by the Forestry Commission. The mansion house became a youth hostel and is now a 25-bedroom hotel sitting in 35 acres of formal gardens and woodland and commanding spectacular views. It is said to be haunted by the ghost of a child, claimed by some visitors to have been seen walking the corridors and descending the main staircase in the early hours of the morning. Others have reported seeing a ghostly image playing in the grounds.

Among the Auchen Castle Hotel's most famous guests were the Beatles. They spent the night there after appearing on stage in Glasgow in the early 1960s at the height of their fame.

TV Pioneer

What's the connection between Craigielands and Coronation Street? The two may seem a million miles apart but the link is Sir Denis Forman, author of *Son of Adam*.

It was under his stewardship at Granada TV in 1960 that the longest-running television soap opera was launched - although he preferred to call it a 'human comedy'.

Sir Denis Forman

The ground-breaking programme which seized top ratings in its first year was just one of many defining productions that Forman brought to the screen. They included the current affairs flagship *World in Action*; the adaptation of Evelyn Waugh's *Brideshead Revisited* in 11 episodes and the lavish 14-part drama *Jewel in the Crown* which set a new standard for classic literary serials.

Forman had already had an action-packed career before joining the Manchester-based TV company where he played a key role for over three decades as effective programme controller and then as chairman.

After Loretto School, he went to Pembroke College, Cambridge, where he took an ordinary degree course in Rural Economy with the long-term intention of buying back Craigielands and running it as a model estate. He missed his final exam but was awarded a pass after obtaining a certificate stating he was ill with a throat infection. He ended up having his tonsils removed in Moffat Cottage Hospital.

World events came crashing down on his plans to return to his ancestral home. After a brief spell in Holland with an import-export firm, he quickly became aware of the inevitability of war and came back to Britain where he was drafted to an officer cadet training unit and then joined the 11 Bn Argyll and Sutherland Highlanders.

Convinced the army was about to fight World War 2 with outdated methods, he dedicated himself to modern military tactics. Promoted to captain, he underwent a month's battle training and became chief instructor at the Battle School at Voxter in Shetland and later its commandant when it moved to Bonar Bridge on the mainland.

In 1943 as a major in the Royal West Kents, he saw action in Italy where he was able to put his tactical theories to the test and found they worked to a large degree. He was involved in recruiting partisans to fight alongside the British Army but his war came to an end at Monte Cassino in March 1944, when his lower left leg was shattered and had to be amputated.

Returning to the UK, he compiled a new Army Manual on infantry instruction, embodying his own views and those of his friend and mentor, Major Lionel Wigram who was killed in Italy.

In 1947 Forman was appointed chief production officer at the Central Office of Information Films. He joined Granada TV in 1955, the year the commercial network was launched, and remained with the company for 32 years, ending as chairman.

In 1990, the second volume of his autobiography *To Reason Why*, charting his army career was published. He also wrote two opera guides - he was deputy chairman of the Royal Opera House, Covent Garden, for nine years - and a book about Mozart's piano concertos.

In 2005, at the age of 87, Forman was presented with the Broadcasting Press Guild's Lifetime Achievement Award for his contribution to broadcasting.

Imperial Medic

Strictly speaking, Dr John Rogerson – personal physician to Empress Catherine the Great of Russia - was not a Kirkparick Juxta man but he lived so nearby that he deserves a place in the parish's hall of fame.

His home in the latter part of his life was Dumcrieff, a mansion at one time rented by the famous road builder John Loudon McAdam.

Rogerson was born in 1741 near Lochmaben and a year after graduating in medicine at Edinburgh University went to Russia at a time when that country was looking westwards and emerging from its cultural isolation. He followed two other Scots doctors, Matthew Halliday and John Mounsey, also both from the Lochmaben area, into a post in the Imperial court.

Soon after his arrival, he won the respect of the Empress by saving the life of the young son of Princess Dashkova, a close friend of Catherine. In 1769 he was appointed court doctor by Imperial decree and given responsibility for the medical care of members of the court.

Seven years after that, Rogerson landed a more important position – Body Physician to the Empress with the rank of Councillor of State. Later he was made a Privy Councillor and became one of the most important men in Russia, living, eating and socializing with the nobility. By all accounts, he was a charmer with all the social graces but was an inveterate gambler.

Catherine, an intellectual and great modernizer of her vast country, had one weakness – men. She compensated for her unsuccessful marriage by taking countless lovers. Rogerson's main duty was to safeguard her from venereal disease, then prevalent in Russia. If she saw a young man she favoured –

Famous Folk

usually an officer – he was first 'tried out' by her ladies-in-waiting. If considered suitable, he then underwent several weeks' instruction on the Empress' likes and dislikes. If he passed muster he was then examined by Rogerson before being allowed into the Imperial bed.

Rogerson returned several times to Scotland during his spell in Russia. In 1782 he was made an honorary member of the Royal College of Physicians of Edinburgh and a freeman of Dumfries.

Yet despite his exalted position and many honours, Rogerson was more a socialite than a skilled medic. Catherine is reported to have described him as

---

One of the most prominent Dumfries citizens in Robert Burns' time was a Kirkpatrick Juxta man.

Gabriel Richardson was born into a farming family at Kellobank in 1759, the same year as the poet. At the age of about 21 he moved to Dumfries and became a prosperous brewer with premises in Nith Place. He became a member of the town council and was provost from 1802 to 1804.

Richardson and Burns were close friends and when the former complained he had to pay an unfair "twa pennies tax" on his ale compared with outside brewers, the poet took up the issue with Provost David Staig in 1793. The tax was adjusted evenly to Richardson's satisfaction and to the advantage of the town's revenue.

Burns wrote a mock epic on Richardson with a diamond on a wine goblet. It was later smashed to smithereens and the exact wording is not known. but it is thought to have gone something like -

> *Here Brewer Gabriel's fire's extinct,*
> *And empty all his barrels.*
> *Ye're blest, if as he brewed ye drink,*
> *In upright, honest morals.*

Richardson had six sons and six daughters. The eldest son John became a surgeon and Arctic explorer who went on two expeditions with Sir John Franklin and on a third to search for Franklin's lost expedition.

Beattock

"a usually fatal doctor" and is to have commented: "I'm afraid anyone who gets into Rogerson's hands is already dead".

He stayed on at court after Catherine's death and when her successor, her son Paul, was assassinated in 1801, he helped his widow to escape, carrying the future Czar Nicolas I in his arms.

Rogerson retired to Dumcrieff in 1816 and died there seven years later aged 82.

I Remember, I Remember...

Old-time residents of Beattock have a deep affection for the area and have fond memories of a rural bygone age. They talk with feeling about the peaceful countryside, the quiet, uncomplicated way of life and the simple pursuits in an era before television, the Internet and package holidays. In the days before the internal combustion engine, provisions like coal, milk and groceries were delivered by horse and cart and other essentials were obtained at the village shop. It as also a more religious time when families still observed a fast day twice a year.

The roots of many of the residents go back to the early days of Beattock and many are descendants of rail, road or farm workers who in the 19th century formed a large percentage of the population. Many families like the Jardines, Borthwicks, Smiths and Saunders have been associated with the village for generations.

Jeannie Wilson, the widow of a rail worker, was born in 1913. As a teenager, she moved from her home in Kirkpatrick Durham, Kirkcudbrightshire, to Beattock to work as a tablemaid with the Hay family in Beattock House.

"They were in shipping in Glasgow and were good to work for," she recalled. "There were five other members of staff - a cook, two housemaids and two gardeners. I can't remember what my wages were but they were quite good at the time. I was off every Thursday and every second Saturday. Beattock was a quiet wee place but there was always something to do. I enjoyed carpet bowling

---

Among Beattock's best-remembered characters are sisters **Maggie and Mearn Hutchison** who ran the village shop at the beginning of last century. Denis Forman, of Craigielands in his autobiographical book *Son of Adam* is highly uncomplimentary to the sisters who, as a child, he hated but he admits Maggie was "an institution revered by grown-ups, trotted out before visitors and called 'the salt of the earth' and 'a great character'".

Beattock resident Margaret Moffat remembers her mother telling her that if any customer in the village shop asked Mearn for pepper, she would automatically sneeze before she even produced it. Ivan Pavlov could have made something of that!

Beattock

and I also liked walking. Sometimes I walked to Moffat or went there on the wee train. In the winter I would go skating on the loch at Craigielands."

One of her most vivid memories is going with other villagers to see the Royal train when it was stopped overnight on the Moffat branch line. "I remember once seeing the young princesses, Elizabeth and Margaret Rose, playing in a field beside the train," she said. "We weren't allowed near them, of course, but I waved and they waved back. Once chap, Dodie Cunningham, sang 'Will Ye No' Come Back Again?' and I thought how silly he was. But the princesses acknowledged him."

Jeannie has one main memory of the war years: the sound of German bombers on their way to blitz Clydebank. "I can still hear the sound," she said. "It was frightening. We were supposed to go to an air raid shelter behind Craigielands but we never bothered."

In her early 20s, Jeannie married John Wilson, a linesman and later a signalman on the railway. His father, also John, had been a coachman at Craigielands.

"The railway was important in Beattock and many of the men worked on it," she said. "It could be hard work. When my husband was a linesmen he would get absolutely soaked. He died of TB."

The Wilsons had two daughters and three sons, one of whom George became a fireman on the banking engines.

Ella Jardine, also born in 1913, - "in the kitchen bed" in the family home beside the village hall - recalled: "I liked living in Beattock. They were happy times and there was lots to do.... there was a youth club with badminton and dancing. I also went to drama classes and took part in performances in the hall. I went to Moffat for piano lessons and attended the Sunday school and bible classes. The Sunday school picnic was held at the big hoose, Craigielands. I liked the games and the cakes. The dog trials on Beattock Hill were also good fun and I remember there was quite a bit of excitement when we went to see the royal train.

"Family walks were a big thing in these days and we used to enjoy strolling up the Evan Water."

Ella whose family occupied the same house for 90 years enjoyed helping with housework and remembers lighting the fire under the boiler for the weekly wash. Paraffin lamps provided the only lighting in the house.

"You could get everything you needed in the shop next to the hall run by Maggie and Mearn Hutchison," she said. "There was a cobbler's across the road, a blacksmith's shop, a joiner's and a soup kitchen near the school run by the headmaster's wife."

Like all Beattock primary school pupils, Ella went on to Moffat Academy and left at 14. During World War 2, she was employed on shift work in the Drungans munitions factory in Dumfries. One of her lasting memories was the VE night celebration in Beattock Hall.

The war years were also recalled by Lex Smith, a brother of Robert, who inspired this book. Born in 1932, he was a schoolboy during the war years and can remember trainloads of troops arriving in Beattock during the night and taking over the steading at Beattock Farm where he lived.

"The place was buzzing in the morning," he said. "The soldiers were paraded in full kit and marched off to Thornhill. The SAS also did manoeuvres in the area."

The village was transformed during the war. There were trenches at the side of the road and two look-out posts – one at the south end of the village and the other at Dyke Farm. Farm workers had to take their turn as lookouts.

Lex also remembers 25lb guns firing at Kinnelhead from their positions on the west side of the railway. "On one occasion a shell fell short and landed near our farm, causing quite a panic but no-one was hurt," he recalled.

Churchill tanks, developed for the British Army after Dunkirk, also carried out exercises in the area. They were too heavy to go over the railway bridge and trundled through the Back Village, demolishing gates and fences.

"One got stuck in the moss and was there for days," he said. "There were also accidents involving Army lorries. I remember a policeman was found dead in the village and it was thought he had been struck by a lorry."

Lex added: "My father started keeping pigs and the Army brought swill to the farm to feed them. I remember thinking how much perfectly edible food was dumped.

"Our farm was originally owned by Beattock House and my grandfather had to supply it with milk, cream and eggs whenever the owners wanted them. No-one in these days would have dreamt of going into the grounds. The lawn was so big the grass was cut by horse and reaper for hay. "

As a youngster Lex had to walk about two miles to Beattock School but other pupils, he recalled, had to trek six miles.

"It was a good school," he said. "The headmaster was Mr Bulman – a superior person and the best master I ever had. He contributed a great deal to the well-being of the pupils. Many of the duxes at Moffat Academy were from Beattock Primary. Everyone had great respect for him. Denis Forman, who criticises him in his book, obviously did not know the man."

Another vivid memory – one shared by many older Beattock folk – is curling on the loch at Craigielands.

"The Smith family who had their business in Liverpool were sent a telegram telling them the ice was thick enough to play and they came up specially," he said. "There were plans to floodlight the loch but it never happened."

One of the Smith family who owned Craigielands – writer Bertram Smith – was a caravan enthusiast and Lex can remember one of them being built.

Beattock

"When they came to take it out of the building, they found it was too big and had to take it apart," he said.

Adam Gray, born in 1920 in Palaceknowe, a mile south of Beattock, had a different sort of war. He joined the local detachment of the Home Guard which, he admits, was "very much like Dad's Army on TV". He said: We mustered in the village hall armed with broom handles. I remember in September 1940, we were ordered to stand-to. Word had come through from Dumfries headquarters that the Germans had invaded. Somebody had got it wrong - which was just as well!"

He was still wearing his Home Guard uniform when he joined the 9th Battalion of the Cameronians early in the war. He was encouraged to choose the regiment by its colonel-in-chief Major-General Sir Eric Girdwood who lived for a while at Marchwoodbank in Beattock "not more than a 3-wood away from the slightly less palatial Gray residence". .

Adam Gray

As a sergeant, Adam saw service from the Normandy landings to the Baltic, and took part in assault crossings of all four major rivers - the Seine, Escault, Rhone and Elbe. At the end of the war, he had the distinction of being the last man to leave the battalion.

Adam, who returned to his job as relief stationmaster at Beattock after demob, has vivid memories of his early years in the village.

"I went to the primary school where there was a headmaster and two teachers," he said. " John Bulman was the head in my time and I'm grateful to him for many things. He introduced me to hockey and cricket. I later played hockey for the Army in Germany and I founded Moffat Cricket Club. I also played football in the summer league.

"There were other sports in the village before the war. The game of quoits was popular and very competitive. There was carpet bowling in the village hall with a big tournament on New Year's Day. Christmas was never celebrated. It was an ordinary working day."

Beattock Show and the sheepdog trials were important events in the rural calendar with almost the whole community taking part - including the children who sold programmes. They both came to an end in the 1930s.

Recalling his schooldays, Adam added: "As youngsters, we had to salute our teacher and doff our caps to the minister. And we had to make our own entertainment. We played with girds and cleeks and in the winter skated on

I Remember, I Remember...

the Craigielands pond or slid down hills on home-made sledges."

James Smith, of Moffat, who was brought up just outside Beattock in the 1920s and 30s, has happy memories of pre-war days in the area but admits life was tough.

"We lived at first in Upper Murthat farm cottage," he said. "My dad helped with the harvest to pay the rent and my mum operated the level crossing gates to let the horses and carts through to the farm. Later we moved to Paleceknowe where there were just six or seven houses.

JAMES SMITH shows a picture of the cottage at Paleceknowe where he used to live.

I remember one family in particular. There were 14 of them. They used to say that the first one up in the morning got the best pair of boots and the best suit. They were a lovely family. The father was a big fat chap. His float used to dip when he sat in it and he sang like a lintie. He made his money by collecting rabbit skins and scrap iron. He was a real character."

As a boy, James did plenty of walking. Every weekday, he walked two miles to Beattock School and the same distance to Sunday school. He thought nothing of driving cattle for three miles on foot from the train to the fields. "As lads we also did a lot of fishing and we used to play pitch and toss," he recalled.

James, who served in Burma with the RASC during the war, added: "I've seen a lot of changes in this area in my lifetime - not all for the best".

In its early days, meetings of the **Women's Rural Institute** in Beattock always held its meetings on the night of a full moon. The date was chosen to ensure members could see their way to the village hall before street lighting was installed in 1950.

The rural, started in 1921 by Lady Younger, was one of the first in Scotland and is still active. During World War 2, the members adopted a trawler and sent parcels to the crew.

Beattock

Everyone living in Beattock in 1993 remembers the night the high-pressure **natural gas pipe** burst open, leaving an 80-foot wide crater.

It disrupted road and rail links for several hours and led to evacuation of about 20 people who spent most of the night in the village hall.

The leak happened on December 22 in a field at Palaceknowe. Nearby residents described a pungent odour and thundering noise " like the roar of a waterfall or an express train" as the gas vented into the night air.

British Gas was alerted around 9pm by its monitoring equipment, police and residents. Although there was little chance of an explosion the A74 trunk road and the West Coast main rail line were closed as a safety precaution. The gas supply was shut down and workmen arrived to inspect the damage at about 11pm

An inquiry by specialists from the British Gas Research and Technology Division revealed that about 1,000 tons of natural gas (valued at £100,000) had been released into the atmosphere.

It was discovered the leak had occurred because the pipe had been realigned earlier that year to make way for the construction of the A 74(M) motorway. A new section of pipe had been installed and protected with a concrete slab. It burst at the point where it was jointed to the original. The experts attributed the failure to overload of the pipeline structure and settlement of the new pipe over an extensive area of infill material.

For Further Reading

Statistical Accounts, Gazetteers etc.
(Old) Statistical Account of Scotland edited by Sir John Sinclair (Blackwood, Edinburgh, 1791-99)
New Statistical Account (Blackwood, Edinburgh, 1834-35)
Third Statistical Account of Scotland: the County of Dumfries (Collins, Glasgow, 1962)
Gazetteer of Scotland Vol. 2 (Chambers, Edinburgh, 1836)
The Topographical, Statistical and Historical Gazetteer of Scotland, Vol. 2 (Fullarton, Glasgow, 1842)
Ordnance Gazetteer of Scotland: A Survey of Scottish Topography, Vol. 4 (Jack, Edinburgh, 1883)
Pigot and Slater: Commercial Directories of Dumfries and Galloway (Dumfries and Galloway Regional Council, 1992)
Transactions of Dumfries and Galloway Natural History and Antiquarian Society - various articles.

Other Books
Adams PWL: A History of the Douglas Family of Moffat and their Descendants (Sidney Press, Bedford, 1921)
Andrew K: The Southern Upland Way - Official Guide Western Section (HMSO 1984)
Brighton S: In Search of the Knights Templar (Weidenfield and Nicholson, 2006)
Caplan N: Border Country Branchline Album (Allan, London, 1981)
Donaldson G: Scottish Historical Documents (Neil Wilson Publishing, Glasgow, 3rd ed., 1999)
Donnachie I and Hewitt G: Dictionary of Scottish History (Harper Collins, 2001)
Drylie JB: Worthies of Dumfries and Galloway (Courier and Herald Press, Dumfries, 1908)
Dunbar AG and IA Glen: Fifty Years with Scottish Steam (D Bradford Barton Ltd., Truro)
Forman D: Son of Adam (Andrew Deutsch, London, 1990)
Forman D: To Reason Why (Andrew Deutsch, London, 1991)
Fraser GM: The Steel Bonnets (Harper Collins, London, 1971)
Gifford L: The Buildings of Dumfries and Galloway (Penguin, London, 1996)
Haldane: Three Centuries of Scottish Posts (Edinburgh University Press, 1971)
Hume JR: Dumfries and Galloway - An Architectural Guide (The Rutland Press, 2000)

Johnson-Ferguson E: Place Names of Dumfriesshire (Courier Press, Dumfries, 1935)

Johnstone CL: The Historical Families of Dumfriesshire and the Border Wars, 2nd ed. (Courier Press, Dumfries, 1889)

Kichenside G: The West Coast Route to Scotland (David and Charles, London, 1976)

McDowall W: History of Dumfries (TC Farries and Co Ltd., Dumfries, Octocentenary ed. 1986)

Mackie JD: A History Scotland (Penguin Books, 1991)

Maxwell, Sir Herbert: A History of Dumfries and Galloway (Blackwood and Sons, 1896)

Prevost WAJ: Annals of Three Dumfriesshire Dales (Herald Press, Lockerbie, 1954)

Reid J: Some Dumfries and Galloway Men (Hunter and Watson, Dumfries, 1922)

Robertson J: The Public Roads and Bridges in Dumfriesshire 1650-1820 (Cromwell, Wiltshire, 1993)

Ross D: Scottish place-names (Berlinn Ltd., Edinburgh)

Russell JA: The Book of Dumfriesshire (Blacklock, Farries and Son, Dumfries, 1964)

Sanders K and Hodgins D: British Railways Past and Present:- South West Scotland (Past and Present, Peterborough, 1903)

Shannon R: Memorials of Kirkpatrick Juxta (Annan, 1973)

Singer J: A General View of the Agricultural State of Property and Improvements in the County of Dumfries (Ballantyne, Edinburgh, 1812)

Smith B: Running Wild (Simpton, Marshall, Hamilton Kent and Co., 1920)

Smith B: Crashie Howe - A Hill Parish (Simpton, Marshall, Hamilton Kent and Co., 1921)

Stell G: Exploring Scotland's Heritage - Dumfries and Galloway (HMSO, 1986)

Thomas D and Whitehouse P: The Romance of Scotland's Railways (Thomas, Nairn, 1993)